You Can't
Teach Until
Everyone
Is
Listening

D1479205

To Alia, with her brilliant personality, playfulness, and humor,
who came into my life unexpectedly and enhances it immeasurably;
to her friend Ocean who is as beautiful in every way as her name;
and to twins Violet and Aria, miracles who make every day a joy and
who take my breath away; Alia, Ocean, Violet, and
Aria, the future is yours.

Source: Photo, art, and production by Dave and Jen Page.

You Can't Teach Until

Teach Until

Everyone

Is
Listening

6 Simple Steps
to Preventing
Disorder, Disruption,
and General Mayhem

Marilyn L. Page   Foreword by
Bruce A. Marlowe

CORWIN PRESS
A SAGE Company
Thousand Oaks, CA 91320

For information:

Corwin Press
A SAGE Company
2455 Teller Road
Thousand Oaks, California 91320
www.corwinpress.com

SAGE Ltd.
1 Oliver's Yard
55 City Road
London EC1Y 1SP
United Kingdom

SAGE India Pvt. Ltd.
B 1/I 1 Mohan Cooperative
   Industrial Area
Mathura Road, New Delhi 110 044
India

SAGE Asia-Pacific Pte. Ltd.
33 Pekin Street #02-01
Far East Square
Singapore 048763

Printed in the United States of America.

Library of Congress Cataloging-in-Publication Data

Page, Marilyn L.
You can't teach until everyone is listening: six simple steps to preventing disorder, disruption, and general mayhem/Marilyn L. Page.
    p. cm.
Includes bibliographical references and index.
ISBN 978-1-4129-6014-4 (copy)
ISBN 978-1-4129-6015-1 (pbk.)
    1. Classroom management. I. Title.

LB3013.P24 2008
371.102′4—dc22   2008006269

This book is printed on acid-free paper.

08   09   10   11   12   10 9 8 7 6 5 4 3 2 1

Acquisitions Editor:	Carol Chambers Collins
Editorial Assistants:	Gem Rabanera, Brett Ory
Production Editor:	Eric Garner
Copy Editor:	Gretchen Treadwell
Typesetter:	C&M Digitals (P) Ltd.
Proofreader:	Charlotte Waisner
Indexer:	Kathleen Paparchontis
Cover Designer:	Lisa Riley

Contents

Foreword

In the spring of 2007, my dear friend and colleague Marilyn Page asked me to consider writing a foreword for a new book she was in the process of completing. I said yes without hesitation. A few months later, the book arrived in my mailbox and when it did, my initial eagerness quickly turned to dread. Another classroom management book? A primer? Teaching is a messy, terribly complex, remarkably unpredictable business. Surely Marilyn knows this, I thought. She is a deep thinker too, one who eschews the formulaic, particularly when it comes to the demands of the teaching profession. The challenges of creating real communities among arbitrary collections of young people forced into a single room; the shared, unspoken sodality between teacher and learner; the difficulty of teaching for understanding: these should not—indeed cannot—be reduced to a simple series of procedures and instructions.

Yet here was Marilyn's book, sitting on my desk, the very title suggesting that just the opposite is true. I was disturbed, but, I must admit, intrigued as well. Did she have a radical change of heart? Did she lose her bearings? The challenge was clear: I had a foreword to write for a book I was pretty sure I did not want to read. My initial anxiety soon led to an increasing sense of trepidation about the whole project, and then an almost intractable procrastination. Truthfully, I did not even crack the book's cover until the urgency of the publisher's deadlines (I missed the first two) and repeated e-mail admonishments started to become embarrassing. Then I read the first page. And the next one and the one after that and before I knew it, I was hooked.

I finished this marvelous little book in one sitting; I imagine you will want to as well. Here, in direct, unadorned prose, is a work of tremendous importance and easy accessibility; a remarkable accomplishment for a number of different reasons, perhaps most notably because the words of an expert teacher are distilled into classroom strategies that are as powerful as they are easy to implement.

Marilyn's considerable wisdom and expertise makes it hard to believe that there was ever a time in her rich and productive teaching career when she "knew nothing," as she tells us in the book's opening pages. She has wide and deep experience teaching young people in every imaginable environment on both coasts and in classrooms in several parts of the interior of our large and multifaceted country. She has taught in rural, suburban and urban schools; in small schools and large ones; and in classrooms with eager students and bored ones, angry students, keen students, those who were cheery and others who were jaded, recalcitrant, and even hostile. She has taught Advanced Placement classes, classes filled with students with disabilities, and in classes where students spoke English as a second (or third or fourth) language. And, for more than twenty years, Marilyn has been a teacher educator too, one who has helped both novices and journeymen. So when she professes that she knew nothing as a first-year teacher it is not an expression of false modesty, but rather an honest appraisal of how she started, how so many of us begin in this most difficult of professions.

Research from my own field indicates that the development of expertise takes time, particularly in professions like teaching where complex information processing is an ongoing requirement. Like authorities in other cognitively demanding fields, expert teachers must commit to memory, and then efficiently organize, large funds of conceptual knowledge before they can smoothly execute even the most routine procedures. In the jargon of educational psychology, expertise develops slowly as declarative knowledge (knowing *that*) evolves into more highly automated procedural knowledge (knowing *how*). But there is an inevitable tradeoff here: as procedural knowledge becomes less attention-demanding and less effortful, it becomes more difficult to explain. (Think about how challenging it is to tell a new driver just how much pressure to put on the gas pedal when shifting into reverse to parallel park.) Put more simply, experts have extraordinary difficulty communicating what they know. And, herein lies Marilyn's great accomplishment: she has overcome this hurdle, skillfully describing the procedures expert teachers use in a way that is so clear that even new teachers can begin practicing them immediately (without having to wait for their declarative knowledge to become overlearned).

In addition to being remarkably clear, useful, and engaging, Marilyn is also unashamedly directive. She has earned the right to be. Marilyn argues here quite forcefully that learning communities do not just happen, that relationships do not form by themselves, that a sense of belongingness and connection requires active, deliberate, and conscious effort on the part of the teacher. In a time of standards and accountability, of renewed concern over declining test scores and student misbehavior, gang activity, and seemingly random violence, how refreshing to be reminded that at the heart of all good teaching is the fundamental importance of building relationships with and between students. To be sure, this is a how-to book, but not of the usual cookbook variety (what Ohanian [2004] has so aptly described as "stir-and-serve" recipes for teaching). Nor is it an animal training guide—masquerading as a book about working with children and young people—whose focus is on proper discipline.

Here the reader will find a thoughtful and explicit handbook for forging relationships and building community. There is none of the usual discussion about rules, nor of the carrot and stick, the "logical" consequences for misbehavior, or the need to punish, embarrass, shame, scold, or even reward. This is not a book about how to correct student behavior or even, as Marilyn claims, a book about preventing misbehavior. It is much more than that. At its root, it is a manual for doing it right, for helping to teach students about getting along, about why that's important, and about how this relates to learning for understanding. As Marilyn notes, students do not, cannot, care about school unless they feel cared about. This is a deeply humanistic book then, disguised as classroom management primer. A book not so much about preventing bad behavior as it is a set of explicit instructions for encouraging, directing—indeed orchestrating—prosocial behavior and the development of classroom community.

Throughout, Marilyn reinforces the very potent, research-based notion that student behavior is directly proportional to teacher behavior, that what teachers do and *how* they do it matters in very important ways. In short, that expert teaching is not accidental; that it is not just the province of "naturals," that teaching expertise develops by practicing what expert teachers do routinely and seemingly without effort. But it is not only a book about what expert teachers do, but also about what they say. That is, Marilyn shows the reader how to use words wisely, why certain words may fail to work as intended, or bore, and instead, when used properly, promote civility, understanding, and connection. And through the use of real classroom vignettes, we come to see quite clearly how the choices teachers make about the very language they use matters in ways great and small, from getting student attention to encouraging inquiry and exploration, from preventing student confusion to promoting independence and increased student-to-student interaction. Marilyn's book is simple, but it is subtle too. Do not be fooled into thinking that this book is only about classroom management, for there are important pointers here, for teachers new and veteran, about extending and deepening student thinking and academic engagement and about increasing independence of thought and critical reflection.

One more thing: You will meet many students in these pages and many teachers too. There are hapless and disorganized teachers, dedicated and highly skilled ones, even some who are just plain dreadful. But in every case, these vignettes tell important stories, capturing in ways both painful and often humorous what it is like to face a classroom of students anxious and waiting to see how things will unfold. Don't skip over these tales, for in them you will be transported into the shoes of real teachers whose experiences provide invaluable lessons.

Marilyn has filled an enormous gap with the publication of this book. It is a guide that is clear and straightforward, but one that affords the reader the same level of respect she so clearly argues teachers should afford their students. Early in the introduction Marilyn asks, "Aren't there already enough books about classroom management?"

There are now.

—*Bruce A. Marlowe, PhD*
Professor of Educational Psychology
and Special Education
Roger Williams University
Bristol, RI

Preface

Knowing Nothing

I knew nothing when I started teaching. Really, I knew nothing. And I knew even less about classroom management. There was a tremendous teacher shortage at the time and schools were hiring just about anyone who breathed. Well, not quite, but almost. I landed my first teaching job only because I had completed two years of college Spanish (I didn't speak a word) and two years of history courses, and Millburg Junior/Senior High School needed someone who could teach both. I had a degree in sociology, no teaching certification, and no teaching experience, but the state issued me a waiver.

It was kind of funny. I was young, looked even younger, and was often mistaken for one of the students. More than once, another teacher approached me as I stood my sentry duty in the passageway between two buildings and told me to get to my room before I was late for class. And my learning about adolescents was on a fast curve. Within a couple of months, I learned about the eighth–grade sex club. It's true—there was an eighth–grade sex club. The girls would wear purple knee socks on Thursdays if they wanted to have sex. That club and other unexpected high jinks tested and twisted my innocence and it was never to be the same.

Mike

I had a particularly difficult student that first year. He was a hyperactive and mischievous ninth grader, who interrupted and disrupted my Spanish class daily and who happened also to be the son of the school superintendent. If anyone had told me at that time that his behavior was my fault, I would have been offended. Instead, being sure he was just a kid out of control, I gave him many after school detentions. This, of course, resulted in self-punishment as I, too, had to stay after school. Did these detentions change his behavior? Maybe, for a very short time, but not really. It definitely didn't ingratiate me with the superintendent.

Two years later, I was working at a different school and one day while driving home, I heard a report on the radio about a teacher who had forced a student to stay in a small closet for a whole period. My outrage was extreme. As I drove along, I was shouting things to myself like "Take away the teacher's certification!" and "Who in their right mind would do that?" and "No student deserves that." My indignation was short lived when, as the report continued, the reporter accidentally named the student while he was explaining that the student's father happened to be the school superintendent. You guessed it. I *knew* this student. It was Mike; it was the student who had joined me in so many after school sessions. In the blink of an eye, my righteous outrage turned to incredible euphoria and a monumental feeling of long overdue retribution. "HooooooooRay!" I now screamed out loud, "Somebody *finally* put that kid in a closet!"

The point of this story is that teaching is not easy. You won't love every student, but you do have to manage a classroom full of them. Managing a classroom is more difficult than teaching, yet essential in order for teaching and learning to occur. There will be 20 to 30 or more students there in your room, all different, all expecting things from you, including, among other things, a safe, positive, and inviting environment.

KNOWING SOMETHING

After several years of teaching in every Grade 7 through 12, at every academic level, and in rural, suburban, and inner city schools, I no longer knew nothing. I knew *something*. Actually, I knew quite a lot. I had had all kinds of extraordinary, surprising, and even shocking experiences including students winning state and national academic competitions; a student hanging himself on a tree outside his parent's bedroom; students overcoming shyness; students sitting in horror as the voice on the intercom announced that President Kennedy was dead; students learning to respect each other; students fighting and falling through plate glass windows; students watching the launch and catastrophic explosion of the Challenger; a student suffering from school phobia actually coming to school; a student being shot; students shooting each other; students threatening to shoot me; students learning to behave responsibly and civilly; students living in their cars and on drugs; and students achieving beyond their wildest expectations and imaginations.

FAST FORWARD TO THE UNIVERSITY— DOING MY HOMEWORK

Yes, I knew a lot, but it took a doctorate and 20 years more, at the university level, of observing and working with K–12 preservice, student, novice, and experienced teachers to figure out what it was that I knew and to put a plan for preventing classroom disruption into words. One state college, two research institutions, and one Jesuit university later, here is how it all came together.

Field Testing: Student Teachers and Videotapes

As a doctoral candidate and for my first 10 years as a college professor, part of my responsibility was to observe student teachers in their practica. I was shocked at how little these student teachers (almost all of whom I had not met before) knew about classroom management, how little preparation they had had in classroom management, and even more shocked at what little initiative they took in developing their own management systems.

From the first time I met the student teachers, I videotaped every class I observed; this was often six times a semester for every student teacher. At the end of a student teacher or intern's first observation, we would discuss, with as much input from the student teacher as possible, what was working and what was not. If that student teacher had little idea of what to do next, I would introduce whichever steps I deemed most necessary for impacting quickly the disarray in that particular classroom. (At the time, I had not identified or named the Six Steps; I just knew what changes had to occur in the classroom.) The student teacher's job was to implement the step(s) from that point forward, consistently and continually. Student teachers responded sometimes with appreciation; often with skepticism; and even with outright resistance, disbelief, and annoyance.

Each subsequent videotape documented what had changed with the application (or sometimes, not) of the particular step(s). At that time, if the student teacher or intern was again not able to figure out himself what he had to do next, I would introduce one (or more) of the other steps, depending on what state the classroom and student teacher or intern were in. In this way, each tape was a documentation of change in the classroom. Over the years, through this process of videotaping student teachers and interns, I accumulated over 1500 videotapes.

Field Testing: Novice and Experienced Teachers

My university work with novice and experienced teachers usually has come about in the process of implementing new programs or new government mandates in the schools; working with participants in major research projects; or, in the case of the Seashore Professional Certification Project in the State of Washington (Page, 1999), directing a pilot project, the purpose of which was to test new professional certification processes and requirements for and with first- to third-year teachers. In the course of these efforts, and from the related data, I have discovered that the novice and veteran teachers I have met who were successfully managing their classrooms were implementing all of the Six Simple Steps and more advanced steps as well. However, there were experienced teachers (sometimes of 20 years or more) who looked like or were even worse managers than the student teachers; the Six Steps were absent; the classes were disorganized, confusing, chaotically loud, unsafe, unfocused, and unproductive. As for the novice teachers, some had figured out a solid classroom management system; the others were floundering and thinking of leaving the profession.

Field Testing: In My Own Backyard

But it wasn't just these experiences and these data that led me to write this book. I don't have to go further than my own Teaching Methods class to find how overwhelmed pre-service teachers are with classroom management issues, even before they set foot in a classroom. For many years at the university, the following scene has repeated itself over and over. On the first day of class (for college sophomores, juniors, seniors, and graduate students, depending on the program) in the teacher preparation methods class, I ask the students to write down the answers to several questions. One of the questions is always, "What is your biggest worry about becoming a teacher?" The answers to that question have been almost all the same and have represented some form of concern about how to manage a classroom full of students—how to keep the classroom safe and calm, and how to know what to do when trouble occurs. At the end of the semester, as the students prepare for their practicums, even though a great deal of time, role-playing, discussion, and practice have focused on classroom management, the same worries resurface and overshadow every other concern about becoming a teacher.

LACK OF TRAINING IN
TEACHER PREPARATION PROGRAMS

There is nothing unusual about any of this. In just about any survey you can find that asks preservice, novice, and experienced teachers about their concerns, classroom management is always on that list and often the most common concern (Gee, 2001; McCormack, 2001). And it is no wonder that pre- and in-service teachers have so many problems dealing with classroom management issues and that they cite this as their main concern in or about teaching. Most teacher preparation programs do not include classroom management courses, and if they do, they are usually elective courses, or not practically oriented, or are relegated to a few class sessions in an education psychology or general methods class (Christiansen, 1996; Evertson & Weinstein, 2006). Novice teachers, especially, often blame their classroom management problems on the lack of related coursework in their teacher education programs (Ladd, 2000) and feel betrayed by those programs (Whitney, Golez, Nagel, & Nieto, 2002). In a study (Christiansen, 1996) of 42 teacher preparation programs, none identified classroom management as a knowledge base included in their training. Some beginning teachers in one study even reported they would have been as well prepared to manage classes if they had skipped all of their college education courses entirely (Davis, 1999).

THE BIRTH OF THIS BOOK

Did you know that 50 percent (often higher in urban areas) of new teachers leave the field within their first five years of teaching (Alliance for Excellent Education, 2005; Bergan, 2007; Darling-Hammond, 2003)? For these novice teachers, and for experienced teachers as well, having problems with classroom management is consistently one of the main reasons they decide to leave the field (Ingersoll & Smith, 2003). Obviously, something has to change. Combining this dismal record with the overpowering amount of data I have collected over many years has led to a percolation in my brain for what has seemed like forever. Until I analyzed all these data, I was mostly working intuitively and looking at a big picture; but it became clearer and clearer that it was Six Simple Steps that were changing and have changed, in dramatic and productive ways, the dynamics of classrooms and the classroom lives of the teachers with whom I have worked.

And so this book, the purpose of which is to describe and explain these Six Simple Steps, was born.

DOCUMENTED RESULTS

It would be silly to suggest that these steps will eliminate entirely all unwanted behavior and disruption in your classroom; there are all kinds of unique and particular issues in different classes. However, the field testing, documentation, and analysis for the work in this book have been extensive. Research methodologies have included both qualitative and quantitative approaches: structured interviewing; phenomenological, 90 minute, in-depth, unstructured interviewing (Seidman, 2006); observation, videotaping and analysis of such (Denzin & Lincoln, 2005); ethnohistorical case study (Page, 1992); surveys; questionnaires; and artifact analysis. The field testing and documentation of 20 years shows that *all* of the preservice and inservice teachers who have used these steps (hundreds of teachers) have had and continue to have substantial success in preventing and reducing unwanted disruption, disorder, and misbehavior in the classroom.

Acknowledgments

Without the hundreds of student teachers and interns who allowed me to videotape their classes, this book would not have been possible. These teachers were willing to listen and to modify what they were doing in the name of creating superior learning environments for their students. They now teach in schools all over the country and many have become teacher leaders. All of you, thank you. You teach, create, and shape the future.

To the novice teachers who had full plates when they met me and still decided to try new approaches, thank you for your patience and determination. Thank you for challenging me constantly.

Thank you also to the experienced teachers who, though often tired and frustrated, agreed, and some reluctantly, to change what they had been doing for several years. I don't think you regretted your efforts. You taught me about persistence and character and vision.

To all the folks at Corwin Press who have assisted me in this journey, thank you. This includes Gem Rabanera, who helped me in every way possible to complete this book; Carol Collins, who stepped into this process after it had begun and knew what to do to get the ball rolling and who has been there with savvy suggestions and encouragement; Brett Ory, who joined Corwin Press when Gem went on to new challenges; Gretchen Treadwell, who respected the integrity of my voice and made copyediting a delight (all authors should be lucky enough to work with Gretchen); to Lisa Riley, who designed a perfect cover; to Eric Garner, who oversaw the production and graciously listened to and worked with my requests; to C&M Digitals (P) Ltd. for the expert typesetting and especially to the typesetter(s) who thought outside the box about the boxes; to Charlotte Waisner, proofreader; and to all other Corwin Press family members who helped with the editing, production, cover, and art work.

Thank you to the peer reviewers who took time out of their busy schedules, read the manuscript, and responded with much positive support and with very helpful critiques.

To Bruce and Bob, master educators, extraordinary scholars, and the most remarkable friends and colleagues, thank you. Bruce Marlowe, a national expert on learning theory and special education, agreed without hesitation to write the Foreword and, then screaming and kicking, finally did; and Bob DiGiulio, a nationally known authority on positive classroom management, reviewed the manuscript with a fine tooth comb and with his brilliant humor, helped me to fix the glaring issues. "Thank you" cannot capture the scope of my gratitude. How lucky are your students! How lucky am I.

Corwin Press gratefully acknowledges the contributions of the following reviewers:

Susan D'Angelo
Teacher, Elementary 5, Gifted/Adjunct Professor
Pineview School for the Gifted/University of South Florida
Nokomis, FL

Robert DiGiulio
Professor of Education
Johnson State College
Johnson, VT

Gail McGoogan
Teacher
Osceola County Schools
St. Cloud, FL

Sharon Roemer
Assistant Superintendent of Instruction
Lucia Mar Unified School District
Arroyo Grande, CA

Devona Rowe
Teacher (AP History/Psychology) (NBCT)
Mandarin High School
Jacksonville, FL

Dana Trevethan
Principal/Adjunct Professor
Turlock High School/California State University,
    Stanislaus
Turlock, CA

Matthew Wight
Principal
Apex High School
Apex, NC

About the Author

 **Marilyn L. Page** is author (with Bruce A. Marlowe) of *Creating and Sustaining the Constructivist Classroom* (Corwin Press, 1998, 2005) and *Creating the Constructivist Classroom*, a six-part video series for grades K–12 (The Video Journal of Education, 1999). She began her career in education as a high school social studies and Spanish teacher and has taught in every Grade 7 through 12, at every academic level, in rural, suburban, and urban school systems in different parts of the United States. She has taught at the university level and worked with pre- and inservice teachers, Grades K–12, for 20 years. She also directed a major and complex research project for the development of K–12 professional certification requirements in the state of Washington. In addition to full-time university teaching responsibilities, she has been the technology coordinator for education programs at two universities and developed the first Middle School Teacher Preparation programs in the Vermont State College System. She earned her EdD from the University of Massachusetts in Amherst in Instructional Leadership and in Educational Media and Instructional Technology. She consults on novice teacher, reform, classroom management, and technology issues in education. She lives in State College, Pennsylvania.

Introduction

It's Not Always About Terrible Students

First, let's start with the important premise that all teachers, to be successful and to have dynamic classrooms, have to be prepared and organized and have to create engaging learning experiences for their students (Winzer & Gregg, 1992). These are critical components in an active and productive classroom. However, teachers can be organized and prepared and provide extraordinary, engaging learning activities and still, easily, sabotage their own classroom dynamic. For 20 years, I have seen this happen repeatedly as I worked with hundreds of student, novice, and experienced teachers, many of whom had worked hours and hours on, and did develop, creative and engaging student learning plans, only to have those plans disintegrate amid classroom disruptions and upheaval.

Almost every one of these frustrated and often depressed teachers, blaming the students for the classroom disarray, has told me how terrible the students are and has warned me: "Wait until you see what they do and how awful they are and then you will understand why there is nothing I can do; they are just horrible kids." Teachers are shocked and often defensive when I tell them that simply by not being proactive in managing their classes, they, the teachers, are contributing to and even causing some of the problems in their classrooms. The real grounding premise here, then, is that it's not about students being terrible; the premise is that teachers have to be proactive.

1

Students and Teachers Have to Feel Safe

The second premise is that students can't learn when they feel unsafe (Crosnoe, Johnson, & Elder, 2004; DiGiulio, 2007; Foundation for a Better Oregon, 2005). Equally important, teachers can't teach when *they* feel unsafe. It is no secret that classrooms out of control are unsafe for everyone, but it doesn't take a drastically chaotic classroom to make students and teachers feel unsafe. All it takes is a small amount of off-task chatting, laughing, smirking, daydreaming, poking, mimicking, or interrupting. A teacher who does not prevent or attend to this disorder appears weak to the students and doesn't earn the students' trust. The students' lack of trust leads to more inappropriate and disruptive behavior and a continual testing of the teacher's ability to run the class; that inappropriate behavior and testing scares students and also the teacher who, in turn, often feels unable to function (Ennis & McCauley, 2002; Irvine, 2003). It becomes a vicious circle of disorder, intimidation, and dysfunction that prevents teaching and learning.

OK, But Aren't There Already Enough Books on Classroom Management?

Teachers need to be proactive and teachers and students need to feel safe; but aren't there enough classroom management books? There is so much written already about classroom management; there are over 20,000 entries in the ERIC database system. Check any college or university library or online bookstore and you will find an enormous selection of books on classroom management. In addition to all the books and articles you can find, there are hundreds of Web sites that mimic the book types. Check Martin's (n.d.) site—it's one of the most comprehensive.

Some of the books are textbooks for college classes; many examine various theories or systems of classroom management; many books provide the strategies for creating a harmonious and productive classroom community; many pride themselves in not being how-to books; some try to address every issue of every classroom in every kind of school and in that attempt describe everything from getting started on the first day of school to planning lessons, arranging the room, using token rewards, speaking to parents, using specific discipline or management programs, and working with the administration.

Some books, unfortunately, look more like how-to books on training animals. They describe and promote techniques such as flicking lights, counting down, ringing bells, giving food and surprise treasures, and heaping praise; others propose and promote similarly reactionary and demeaning actions such as putting names on the board or in a fish bowl; timing out; putting color chips on desks; declaring "do this and you'll get that"; putting students in the corner facing the wall; forcing students, in the corner, to read and reread the rule(s) they violated; and an unbelievable array of other such behaviors. Some books (DiGiulio, 2007), thankfully, try to move away from the unproductive and often degrading reward and punishment system, which, at best (Kohn, 1993), leads to temporary behavior adjustment, rarely works long term, and seldom addresses root causes.

So Why Another Book, and What Is Different About This Book?

This is not your typical book about classroom management. This book is a primer and it *is* proudly and unabashedly a how-to book. This book is simple and clear. It distills years of research, data, and the experiences of hundreds of pre- and inservice teachers into six simple, necessary, and doable steps for managing your classroom. It is not a book about reward and punishment; it is a book that shows teachers, through the stories of others, how to prevent classroom disruptions, not how to react to them. At the same time, it is much more, because it demonstrates how implementing these Six Steps allows teachers to focus on the real issues and challenges: creating alive and productive classrooms that hum with positive energy, and helping students to grow and learn to their greatest potential. Most important, the Steps work. They can be lifesavers for teachers who don't know where to begin with managing their classes and the solution for teachers who have read about, tried, and become disillusioned with other proclaimed systems.

It is the book that professors who are teaching in teacher preparation programs can introduce to their preservice students. It is the book every new teacher can carry into the classroom—first to the practicum and then into the real world; it is the book every novice and experienced teacher who struggles with classroom issues needs because it is never too late to change the climate and culture of a classroom. This book is meant to be carried with you, crumpled from use, and to result in very shocking and positive changes in your classroom and in your confidence as a classroom leader.

THE TITLE

The title, *You Can't Teach Until Everyone Is Listening*, captures the core of the book. It does not refer to any particular kind of teaching or learning approach. It definitely doesn't refer to standing in front of a class and lecturing. The key word in the title is "everyone" and what the title means is that little, if any, meaningful teaching or learning can occur if the teacher and the students are not paying attention.

The Teacher

If the teacher is oblivious to student disruptions or misbehavior in the class, or sees it but ignores it for lack of knowing what to do or perhaps for fear of worse disruptions, then students cannot learn. If the teacher is not "listening" to the heartbeat and dynamic of the class, student and teacher accomplishments will be stunted at best.

The Students

On the other hand, if the students are not attending and not "listening," because they are misbehaving themselves or there are too many distractions, or they feel unsafe in the classroom or the teacher is a poor class manager, then they will not be very successful. Instead, they will be frustrated, lack respect for the teacher, tune out, or even create more mischief.

THIS BOOK'S STRUCTURE

The Vignettes

In this book, there are 14 vignettes that introduce different contexts, teachers, schools, students, and issues. The vignettes illustrate and humanize the issues and provide working examples of implementing the Six Simple Steps. The people, schools, and events in this book are real. All names are pseudonyms. Whether a vignette features a student, novice, or veteran teacher, and whether the vignette represents Grade 2 or Grade 4, Grade 8 or Grade 10, or an inner city school or a rural school, a small school or a big school or a school with great diversity or almost none, there are lessons for all teachers in each vignette. From these scenarios, elementary, middle, and secondary teachers, whether pre- or inservice and regardless of content area, can learn why and how these Six Simple Steps can make a difference.

The Chapters

Each of the first six chapters describes and explains one of the Six Steps. The last two chapters focus, respectively, on a model for reclaiming a chaotic class and on how teachers at any career stage can use these Steps.

- Chapter 1 explains how knowing and using the students' names consistently, constantly, fluidly, and without hesitation, prevents disruption and leads to greater student attention, interaction, and focus. Additionally, it speaks to the importance of students knowing and using each other's names.

- Chapter 2 defines anonymous and dangling questions. It discusses why and how using such questions usually leads to chaos in a classroom, and how asking questions differently can eliminate disorder and lead to productive thinking and responding.

- Teacher language is the focus of Chapter 3, which examines two sides of the coin: the detrimental results of using unnecessary filler or unprofessional words in teaching and the positive impact of using civil language in creating productive and safe classroom environments.

- Chapter 4 focuses on how to give directions and instructions in ways that avoid student confusion, require students to pay attention, prevent classroom disruption, and allow and cause students to get and stay on task.

- Chapter 5 first explains why different classes need different amounts and kinds of attention and then describes what to do to prevent student distraction and general unruliness when there is a transition or new task in the classroom.

- Chapter 6 speaks to the importance of interacting with all students multiple times every day to build teacher-to-student connections. It also explains how to develop and increase student-to-student connections and relationships in order to create class cohesiveness, wholeness, and energy while simultaneously and consequently reducing disorder.

- In Chapter 7, two teachers provide models for bringing disorderly, chaotic, and dysfunctional classrooms back to a place where it is possible to begin to introduce the Six Steps. These are models for teachers whose classes are already in too much disarray to begin to make productive changes.

- Chapter 8 presents ideas on how you can implement and use the Steps depending on where you are in your career. There are suggestions for preservice, student, novice, and experienced teachers as well as for university professors.

A Word About Labels

It has become increasingly difficult to find acceptable descriptors when referring to a person's ethnic, racial, or cultural connections. It seems as though everyone has an idea about what is correct and what is not. Different parts of the country have their own preferences about these labels as do members of the same groups.

One colleague who is of Native American heritage wants never to be called *Native American*. She prefers *American Indian*. While *Hispanic American* is popular in some literature and some areas of the country and even in Wikipedia, many people who have roots in Latin America prefer *Latino*. *Anglo American* has become synonymous with *White* in some literature and in conversations. Some *Pacific Islanders* don't mind being called *Asian,* others do. Some folks of African heritage prefer *Black*; others prefer *African American*; still others prefer *people of color.*

I have chosen to use the terms *White, Black, American Indian, Indian, Asian,* and *Latino* to refer to any generation American, whether first, second, or other. These names indicate the heritage of the people described.

Before You Implement the Steps: Providing Explanations

Before you begin, consider that part of the students' feeling of safety in a class comes from knowing why you, the teacher, are doing what you are doing and what you are going to do next and why. Whether you are at the beginning of a school year or somewhere in the middle or even near the end of the year, explaining your actions and changes in classroom processes and procedures, and reasons for such, goes a long way to developing understanding, calmness, clarity, and feelings of security for everyone.

Each of the Six Simple Steps, some of which may seem *too* simple (don't be fooled), plays an important role in developing a safe, secure, organized, calm, productive, and positive classroom environment; there are reasons for each of the steps and you may have additional explanations to add. It would be a tactical error to omit the explanations for the changes or processes connected to these steps, no matter what the students' ages or grade levels. Knowing is safe. And once you have explained the reasons, students are more ready to cooperate, and you are ready to take and implement the Step.

THE ROADMAP

The Six Simple Steps provide the roadmap that allows every teacher to become a successful classroom manager. While it would be ideal if all teachers were able to have identical levels of success when implementing these Steps, life isn't that perfect. Not all teachers are created equal and no two students or groups of students are the same. The infinite number of variables that emerge within a classroom and in a school preclude carbon copy experiences. No teacher should be discouraged, though, if the first try at implementation of a step is less than perfect. Persistence, determination, focus, and even revisiting a particular step will make the difference.

And remember, being able to manage your classroom successfully is not the end of the journey; it is the beginning.

1

The Critical Beginning

Knowing and Using Students' Names

BARRY

The Context

Barry was a senior in a secondary teacher preparation program at a large research university. His student teaching assignment was at North High School, which was located in a small suburban city of approximately 20,000. One of his classes was tenth-grade civics and that was the first class I visited after Barry had completed his preliminary classroom observations. Barry had been teaching the civics class for two weeks at that point. All of his students were White and were academically heterogeneous.

Barry's Plan

Barry had decided that every Friday would be a current events day and that each student would find a newspaper article representing a contemporary political or social issue to analyze and present to the class. During the presentation, the other students in the class would develop three critical questions they would ask at the end of the presentation. This seemed like an acceptable, though not particularly creative, plan.

Friday

Students entered the room several at a time. Most were talking among themselves and carrying bursting backpacks slung over their shoulders. They slumped into their seats like rag dolls and, with a thud, dropped their bags on the floor. Barry sat behind his desk at the front of the room and never looked up and never spoke. When the bell announced the beginning of class, without attempting to get the students' attention, and apparently without even noticing whether or not he had their attention, Barry launched into directives about how the day's class would go. He then walked to the back of the room, parked himself at a desk in the last row, and said, "Justin."

Justin

A tall, lanky 16-year-old with a sour look on his face dragged himself up to the front of the room as if he were heading for the gallows. He leaned forward on top of the podium and in a monotone read his article to the class without once glancing from the paper. It was dreadfully boring and had nothing to do with current events. Part way through the reading, students began to engage in distracting side conversations. Barry paid no attention to those chatting students, to Justin's demeanor, or to his article content.

The Questions

At the conclusion of Justin's presentation, Barry tried to prompt students to ask their questions by saying, "It's time for the questions." When there was no response from anyone, Barry let loose with a string of five questions himself. He made no eye contact with anyone, including Justin. From his own notes, he read questions he had developed during Justin's reading and again paid no attention to the escalating problem of student distractions, which included talking, sliding back-packs between desks, passing notes, and eating. He didn't reply to Justin's responses. He plowed on with his questions.

After Justin

When Barry had finished asking his questions, he announced that Justin could sit down and the person in the first seat in the first row would go next. This pattern of each student getting up to the podium in order of seating, reading an article, often as he leaned over the podium, of no students asking questions, and of Barry asking a flurry of questions, continued for the entire period. By the time the class ended, Barry's voice had gotten louder and louder so he could talk over the escalating din in the classroom. The only name Barry had used during the entire class was "Justin."

Student Presentations

Unfortunately, student presentations can be uninspiring, lack substance, represent little learning or analyzing on the part of the student presenter or the rest of the class, and, additionally, evoke all kinds of undesirable, off-task behavior in the class. Try an alternative. Instead of requiring a talking and listening event, which is a setup for student misbehavior, ask each student to "conduct a learning experience" with the class. This would require each student to demonstrate his or her own understanding while involving other students in an activity or activities through which they can learn about the concept or topic. Any age student can do this at some level. It takes your expertise to shift students' expectations of their roles and your guidance to show the students how to do this. One way to begin is to ask for the students' ideas on how this can happen. (See Marlowe & Page, 2005, for more information.)

While Barry's story includes many classroom management issues that typically can be present during a student or new teacher's first few weeks of teaching, there is one

Classroom Management Issues

What issues of classroom management can you identify in Barry's scenario?

Review the issues listed at the end of the chapter to determine how your issues match.

issue that is the most critical of all for any grade teacher, whether student, novice, or experienced, and it is this issue that needed the most attention before Barry could proceed successfully. What is the issue and what happened to Barry?

KNOWING AND USING STUDENTS' NAMES

Whether you define your class and teaching approach as traditional, teacher-centered, student-centered, progressive, inquiry-based, project-based, Socratic—or anything else— for optimal learning to occur, the classroom has to be a safe and caring place and students need to feel that they belong (Charles, 2000; Crosnoe et al., 2004; Irvine, 2003; Jones & Jones, 2004). Regardless of who they are or what their backgrounds are (Schlosser, 1992), students won't care *about* school unless they feel cared about *at* school. The first of the Six Simple Steps provides the grounding for the development of a positive and caring classroom environment by creating initial and important ongoing interaction with students.

As simple and as obvious as it seems, knowing and using students' names is critical and indicates to the students that:

1. You care enough to make the effort.

2. You care enough to interact with them on an individual basis and want to get to know them.

3. You know what you are doing and are confident.

4. They are not anonymous.

5. They do not intimidate you.

YOUR NUMBER ONE
CLASSROOM MANAGEMENT TOOL

Wait . . . Teachers already do this, don't they? Teachers usually, although not always, do know and use their students' names. What makes knowing and using students' names a classroom management tool is how quickly teachers learn the students' names at the beginning of the school year (or practicum) and the speed, ease, and frequency with which teachers use the names at the beginning of and throughout the year (or practicum). But just as important for establishing a positively functioning classroom is that the students know and use each others' names as well and as quickly as the teacher does. When students feel anonymous or disconnected from other students or the teacher, random misbehavior occurs easily; conversely, when students feel connected to the teacher and other students, it becomes much less likely that they will disrupt the class (Dornbusch, Erikson, Laird & Wong, 2001). There is a difference in how this process of knowing and using student names can happen for pre- and inservice teachers.

STUDENT TEACHERS AND INTERNS

There are many different ways in which preservice teachers begin their practica. Some begin on the first day of the school year; some begin in January after the classroom teacher and students have established routines (good or bad); some begin five or six weeks into the term in a prepracticum; in some field-based teacher preparation programs (Clark et al., 1989), the interns become and assume all responsibilities of a classroom teacher immediately. Regardless of when a student teacher or intern begins a practicum or internship, learning and using the students' names is still the most critical step in classroom management, in preventing minor disturbances as well as chaos, and in developing a classroom environment that becomes a petri dish for learning.

Before the Teaching Practicum Begins

Many practicum programs require that the student teachers or interns spend the first few weeks in the internship completing focused observations and occasionally assisting the mentor teacher with such tasks as copying papers, preparing Power-Point slide shows, developing a student learning center, accompanying students to the library, and delivering messages to the office. Some universities even require that the student teachers spend time visiting other classrooms and programs in the school. While these are important exercises in getting familiar with the classroom and school community, these requirements can make it difficult to learn and use the students' names quickly. But learning the students' names *is* what you need to do. By the end of the first day in the practicum, you as a student teacher or intern should be able to match a name with a face and should have had verbal interaction, using the student's name and eye contact, with every student.

Each subsequent day until you take over the class, find a way to interact with each student. It could be as simple as standing at the doorway and saying, "Hello, Oneeka"; Hello, Garcia"; "Good Morning, Britt"; and continue until you have welcomed by name every student in the class. These greetings also could include a variety of expressions such as,

Name Tags

Name tags are one easy way to ensure this daily interaction and name learning.

"I missed you yesterday." or "How did the soccer game go?" or "How is your project going?" or "Are you feeling better?" or "I am happy to see you."

Student Teacher's Responsibility

Knowing the students' names on the first day may not be on your list of university requirements. Your professor at the university may not think this is critical or simply may not have thought about it. In this case, you have to take the initiative; be proactive and explain to the mentor teacher why you need and want to do this. Be persistent, yet respectful. Some teachers may suggest you'll get to know the names in due time; others may say there is not time. Again, be persistent (Who can object to name tags?). You will save yourself and the class from much of the mischief that often occurs when student teachers take over the class. The students will know that you know them; they will respect your confidence; they will believe that you know what you are doing; they will believe that you care; and they will know they are not scaring you. You already will have developed the beginning of important teacher-student connections. Once you take over the class, interact with every student every day. At that point, it will be necessary to begin to develop the student-to-student connections described below.

In field-based programs in which the intern becomes the full-time teacher immediately, and sometimes without a mentor, the job is the same as for any other full-time teacher. Know and use the student names fluently by the end of the first day at the elementary level and require the same of the students. At the middle and secondary level, be fluent in using names by the end of the second week.

NOVICE AND EXPERIENCED ELEMENTARY TEACHERS

For novice and experienced elementary teachers, there is no excuse not to learn and use students' names on the first day of school. By the end of the first day, be able to match the names to the faces without hesitation; and to interact with each student multiple times during that first day using the student's name as you make eye contact. This is more important than anything else you do on that first day of school. It will save you hours of having to attend to disorder that will occur in the classroom as the year progresses if you don't do it.

There are several ways to go about this. Review the class roster before school begins. Get familiar with the names in the class. On the first day of school, the easiest and most foolproof method of learning the names is to have name tags prepared for students. Have them wear the tags for most of the day, then test yourself. By the end of the day, be able to use each student's name correctly without the name tags. On the second and subsequent days, make your first order of the day to name each student while having direct eye contact with that student.

Because student-to-student interaction is just as important as teacher-to-student interaction, begin to work on it the first day and each subsequent day for about two weeks. Ask different students each day to name all the students while they are making eye contact with the students they are naming.

Aito

Not all elementary teachers have the luxury of seeing their students every day, all day. Consider Aito. When I met Aito, he was a 10-year veteran, physical education teacher in a K–6 school with a population of 650 students. The school was located in one of the largest school systems in the nation and housed such a diverse population that the school handbook came in seven languages.

The Upside of Aito's Schedule

Aito taught physical education to every student in the school so that as his students moved up grades, they tended to grow as a family. Once he had established connections with and among the students in the lower grades, processes became more and more fluid. Less and less time had to be spent on learning students' names and on classroom management issues.

The Downsides of Aito's Schedule and Class Size

But the year I met Aito, in one of his third-grade classes, he had 39 students, 9 of whom were emotionally disturbed; there was one aide in the gym with Aito. The students who were emotionally disturbed displayed a variety of antisocial behaviors that needed constant attention of one kind or another. But in terms of getting to know his students, it was Aito's schedule that was the biggest problem. He only met with each class twice a week for an hour. Sometimes, this lack of continuity was a barricade to ongoing connections with and among students. Each class tended to need reminders and renegotiation of communication and interaction processes and policies.

The other problem involved students new to the school. By the third grade, Aito's students knew each other fairly well and had formed a closely knit unit. A new student entering one of his classes was faced with how to get to know the other students and become and feel like a part of the group.

Shalee

Shalee was a new student in this third-grade class. Aito had enough experience to know that, regardless of how seldom his classes met, without the students getting to know and interact with each other, there would be more rather than fewer behavior issues. His method of introducing students to each other was to use ice-breaking games. That is what he tried to do on this first day to help Shalee feel welcome.

While the other students ran to the center of the gym to join in the game, Shalee clung to the wall like glue. The class got rather noisy because some of the students with special needs had little self-control and tended to shout profanities at a fairly regular clip. Shalee began to cry.

Getting to Know Shalee

Aito stopped the class and very quietly talked to the students about their responsibility in welcoming new class members. He asked some of the noisier students to go with the aide to another section of the gym to complete a particular exercise and then spoke very briefly to Shalee assuring her that it was all right to sit on the sidelines until she felt ready to join the other students. After a short time, he sent two of his students over to the wall where Shalee was. Their job was to make Shalee feel welcome. Their previous experiences in Aito's classes informed them on how to do this. They had learned how to talk about things they might have in common, and after three previous years with Aito, they had become quite skilled in group processes and in helping new students to learn names.

Meanwhile, Aito restarted the game and after a short time, sent two more students over to Shalee so that they could introduce themselves to her as the previous two returned to the game. They were all familiar with how this procedure worked. Aito continued to send students to Shalee at staggered intervals and before the end of the hour, the entire class had introduced themselves to Shalee.

The Results

The next class was two days later and Shalee was still not quite ready to move freely into the class. Once again, Aito asked two students at a time to spend time with her. He repeated this procedure for several more classes and eventually Shalee felt comfortable enough to join in without hesitation. Aito's class was ready to move forward as an integrated group.

Novice and Experienced Middle and Secondary Teachers

Preteens and Teens

At the middle and secondary schools, knowing and using student names is even a more critical and more complex undertaking. Preteens and teens are fascinating. Even more than with elementary students, the middle and secondary classroom environments are affected by the safety and sense of belonging a student feels (Blum, McNeely, & Rinehard, 2002; Cothran & Ennis, 2002; Nieto, 1999; Schlosser, 1992). Teens and preteens come to school in a variety of conditions. In different degrees and at different times, feelings of alienation and being disenfranchised can be common; many students are dealing with social and physical differences and issues; cognitive development and hence the ability to argue can kick into high gear; some students are abusing drugs; many high school students are working 40 hours a week; and peers become ultimately more important support groups than family.

These and other developmental and cultural factors impact the behavior of middle and secondary school students and consequently the dynamics of their classrooms. These factors even impact how teens and preteens *enter* the classroom; for preteens, it can be a lot of pushing, slapping, shoving, and tripping (playful or otherwise) and for teenagers, it can range from a tidal wave, tornado, or a volcano-like process (see Chapter 5) to a lethargic and dreary funeral march. It takes a skilled teacher to manage it all and provide a positive, productive, and safe classroom environment. Indeed, middle and secondary students are fascinating . . . and needy.

The Middle and Secondary School Day

Additionally, there are procedural and number differences (Emmer & Gerwels, 2006) that change the nature of classroom management and safety issues at the middle and secondary level:

1. Students usually move from one class to another several times a day.

2. Students face different sets of rules, processes, procedures, and requirements in every class.

3. There is a lag of up to 24 hours (or sometimes three days if there is block scheduling) between the set of rules and procedures in class A until the student is back in class A again with that same set of rules. In between that time period, they may have worked with five or more other sets of rules and procedures.

4. A middle or secondary teacher might have between 70 and 150 students every day—approximately 5 to 10 times the number of names the elementary teachers have to learn and only one-fifth the time daily with each group.

Learning the Names

Take the entire period for each class on the first day of school to learn and use the students' names. You can find many strategies for learning names on the Internet, but one of the easiest is also the most productive, because students have to learn everyone's name at the same time you do. So not only are you and the students learning each other's names, the process is the beginning of making connections and changing a group of individual students into a cohesive and consequently less problematic class. Remember to explain why learning names is important.

An Easy Strategy

1. Explain to the students that they are going to be in pairs and will ask each other two questions. (Create your own questions, if you don't like these. You can be more inventive and match the questions to the students, age, and grade.) Then each member of the pair will introduce the other to you and the class by name and with the responses to the questions. For example: "This is Laura. Her favorite subject is science and her favorite movie is *Surviving Frank*."

2. Have the questions on the board:
   a. "What is your favorite school subject?" (Replace with your question.)
   b. "What is your favorite movie or TV show or hobby?"

3. Before they begin to introduce each other, remind them (especially the middle school students) that everything they say has to be acceptable in a school setting.

4. Also mention to them that when the process is complete, you will ask two students to name every student in the class; this will encourage them to pay attention more intently.

5. If the students you choose cannot remember all the names, ask the student in question to say her name or ask another student to assist in naming the student and then let the original student continue.

6. Once two of the students have named everyone, then it is your turn. Looking at each student, say the name. If you can't name some of the students, this is your chance to ask that student his name. You then repeat it and try it all over again. This will establish your desire to know each student as an individual and the students will recognize your strength and presence, a necessary ingredient in the classroom management recipe.

Probably this will be the only thing you can accomplish on the first day in each class. It will be well worth your effort. Most likely, in the second class you will forget some of their names, especially if it is not a daily class. Start each class for the next two weeks by asking two students to name each student, followed by you naming all the students. This will get faster each day and by the end of two weeks, you and the students should have the names and faces connected and the names at the tips of your tongues. Don't worry about class work until this is accomplished. It is the most critical foundation for your class environment and for students being productive in the classroom.

OTHER APPROACHES

The Seating Chart

Once you have completed these exercises, as a backup support, use a seating chart. There is nothing wrong with holding that seating chart to get the names right, after you have gone through the previous exercise. There is everything wrong with thinking holding a seating chart is lame and that not using the students' names is OK. You will pay for those mistakes over and over throughout the year. This is all about establishing contact, connections, awareness, your role and status in the classroom, and the beginning of classroom interactivity and a sense of community. Without being able to use and without using the students' names every single time you address a student, you will have sent the messages to them that you don't care enough to bother, that they are not important to you, that you aren't paying attention, that you are tired, that they intimidate you, or that you are not the leader. These are not the messages you want to send if you want your students to behave, respond, and engage positively and energetically.

Name Tags and Name Signs

Another backup approach following the initial exercises is to use name tags or have the students fold over a 3 × 5 index card, write their names with a very large black marker, and place the card as a tent at the front of the desk or table. To increase student-to-student interaction, have the students place the name signs in a box at the end of the period; for the next several days, ask different students to hand out the signs at the beginning of class.

Block Scheduling

There are several different kinds of block scheduling at the middle and secondary grades. Some block scheduling presents the same issues that Aito had in his third-grade physical education class in that the students may only meet once, twice, or three times a week. If you work in one of these formats, it is even more critical to repeat these exercises until you and all students know, can, and do use each other's names.

BACK TO BARRY

The View From the Back of the Room

What I saw from the back of Barry's room was a class that lacked soul, had no sense of community, had little student engagement or focus, had much too much distracting behavior to allow for learning or a feeling of student safety, and had almost no teacher-to-student connections. The most important thing Barry needed to do before proceeding with the academic curriculum and before being able to address the other classroom management issues was to learn and use the students' names. He needed to welcome the students into his classroom by name, he needed to call them confidently by name once they were in his classroom, and he needed to interact with all of them throughout the class. Without this critical beginning step, Barry's lesson plans were running amuck. Things deteriorated quickly and drastically in the class. The students began to heckle and mimic Barry every time he talked as if to cry out, "We are here. Get to know us. Recognize us. Talk to us. Yoo-hoo, over here. *Hello. . . . ?*" Barry droned on seemingly oblivious to them and their behavior.

What Happened to Barry?

Unfortunately, Barry was unable to learn and use the students' names to any reasonable degree. He was also unable to make eye contact with students. Without this necessary foundation, he could not connect with students on an appreciable level and could not accomplish much academically. Additionally, because he lacked these important connections with the students, attempts at classroom management were futile; every day, in every class, mayhem reigned. About half-way through his practicum, Barry resigned and forfeited his certification.

Without knowing and using the students' names consistently and constantly, you, too, will undermine your own hard work as Barry did. But this doesn't have to happen. Become skilled at knowing and using the students' names and you will be on your way to creating a classroom dynamic that reduces disorder and disruption and increases classroom safety and on-task behavior.

Barry's Classroom Management Issues

1. *Barry's lack of verbal and eye contact with students as they entered the room.*
2. *Barry's lack of interaction with students during class.*
3. *Barry's lack of awareness of and attention to student distractions and rude behavior during student presentations.*
4. *Barry's lack of attention to his own directions and assignment requirements.*
5. *Barry's lack of checking for understanding with students before beginning presentations.*

SUMMARY: STEP 1

1. Learn students' names either before or on the first day of school.

2. Every class for the first two weeks, ask different students to name all the students. You do the same.

3. If you need assistance in remembering the names, use name tags, seating charts, or 3 × 5 tent cards on desks or tables.

4. Interact with each student by name several times a day at the elementary level and at least twice a period at the secondary level.

WHAT COMES NEXT?

Chapter 2 focuses on something that teachers do just about every day in just about every classroom; that is, asking questions. It explains what anonymous and dangling questions are, why and how using them can lead to chaos in a classroom, and how teachers can ask questions in more productive and less disorganized ways.

2

Avoiding Anonymous and Dangling Questions

Dave

The Context

Dave was married with two children, ages six months and six years, when he decided to give up his job as a computer programmer to become a teacher. He enrolled in the graduate program at his local state college where he was not only an exemplary student, but also became a popular leader on campus and a DJ for the college's radio station. After two years of classes, he felt very ready to begin his practicum in a seventh-grade earth science classroom at a K–12 public academy in a very small (population approximately 3700), rural-suburban, middle socioeconomic town. The town and student population were 100 percent White.

Dave's Problem

Dave's first two weeks were fairly quiet as his mentor stayed in the room with him assisting in the work and providing advice when needed. As Dave reported, and as often happens, when the mentor left the room on a semi-permanent basis, things went downhill quickly. The students spun out of control with disrespectful behavior to both Dave and the other students. Some yelled out responses loudly and impatiently whenever Dave asked a question, others paid no attention, some poked and disturbed others, and some made derogatory remarks to no one in particular. Dave felt the class slipping away from him. When it was time for me to observe Dave's class, he called me the night before to warn me that he had "awful kids" and that nothing he tried was having any positive effect. "Wait until you see how terrible they are," he reminded me twice.

My presence in the classroom prompted no change in the students' behavior, but I did know in the first few minutes of the class what the problem was. These were not "awful kids." They were normal 12- and 13-year-olds. Was Dave doing, or not doing, something that was contributing to or even encouraging the student misbehavior and chaos?

The Lesson

Students had been studying the earth's water cycle, and at the beginning of the class, Dave asked, "Did everyone complete the homework?" I could hear two or three students respond with a "yes." The rest made no response.

"Good," Dave proclaimed, "take your homework out and refer to it as we review these questions." With a symphony of rattling and rustling, students pulled papers out of their backpacks and slapped the papers on their desks.

Dave, assuming all was well with the homework, moved on with the class by pulling down a precipitation map of their state and firing off a question: "Which area of the state gets the greatest amount of rain?" A few students yelled out answers.

"Great," Dave responded. He pointed to a particular location on the map and threw out another question, "How much rain does this area get?" The same students yelled out answers. He praised them again. As he asked the next questions in rapid succession ("Which area gets the least amount of rain?" "Why is there such a difference?" "How do the mountains impact the amount of rain?"), he got the same results each time from the same students and he responded with the same kind of superficial praise.

And the Rest of the Class?

What began to happen in the rest of the class was what he had described to me the night before. The students not involved in answering Dave's questions began to misbehave or withdraw. A couple of students put their heads down on their desks, two others started to poke each other, three or four students were sliding their desks and chairs around as if they were bumper cars, and some were purposefully dropping pens on the floor. If the students weren't engaged in distracting behavior, they were simply not paying attention. In the midst of asking questions, Dave tried to address these behaviors and even reluctantly sent one student to the principal's office, but overall he had little effect on the students' antics.

Before analyzing Dave's dilemma, the cause of the chaos, and the remedy, we need to examine the kinds of questions teachers often ask students.

TYPES OF QUESTIONS TEACHERS ASK

Teachers ask students questions for different reasons. One purpose could be to determine student command of important information; another could be to determine student understanding of concepts or processes; still another could be to prompt students to think and solve problems. There are four *types* of questions that teachers tend to ask their students.

Type 1

Type 1 questions look for and expect "yes" and "no" answers. For example:

- Is Boston the capital of Massachusetts?
- Is oil heavier than water?
- Is today Tuesday?
- Did Shakespeare write *The Importance of Being Earnest?*

Type 2

Type 2 questions are "who did it" and "who is it" questions, which lead to short and usually one-word answers. For example:

- Who is Harry Potter?
- Who is the President of the United States?
- Which country in Europe has a time period called the White Nights?
- Who discovered the cure for polio?

Type 3

Type 3 questions are "what is (are)" and "where is (are)" questions which, similarly to type 2 questions, lead to short or one-word answers. Consider these:

- What is the capital of Illinois?
- Where is the Nile River?
- What is 2 + 7?
- Where in the United States will you see the bald eagle?

Type 4

Type 4 questions are "why" and "how" questions that look for and encourage reasoning, critical thinking, and investigation. Consider the following:

- Why do leaves turn color?
- How can 2 plus 2 *not* be 4?

- Why did the North win the Civil War?
- Why is the ocean blue?
- How did you come to that solution?

LEVELS OF QUESTIONS TEACHERS ASK

Besides the four different *types* of questions, there are also two different *levels* of questions.

Lower Level Questions

Question types 1, 2, and 3 are lower level questions. Lower level questions lead to little, if any, thinking or understanding. Instead, they:

1. Encourage and in fact force students to find "right" answers and essentially they infer that there *are* right answers.

2. Often require student memorization.

3. Lead the students to be dependent on the teacher—not only for confirmation of the answer, but also for praise.

Lower level questions often lead to students trying to please teachers rather than to thinking independently and at a higher level (Gardner, 1991; Kohn, 1993).

Higher Level Questions

Type 4 questions, such as "How did you come to that solution?" lead to higher level thinking and require students to find, use, connect, analyze, and interpret information in some way. These kinds of questions are necessary if students are to become the thinkers and creators we need to sustain a democratic way of life. However, type 4 questions can have the same problem as the others; that is, many teachers use type 4 questions in such ways as to encourage and often require student dependency on the teacher for the ultimate "right" answer.

The purpose here, though, is to figure out how to *manage* your class when asking questions. Using dangling and anonymous questions is not the way to manage a class. Dangling and anonymous questions—of whatever type and whether they are lower or higher level—lead to yelling out, distraction, annoyance, lack of attention, general mayhem, zoning out, and lack of learning.

DANGLING QUESTIONS: WHAT ARE THEY, AND WHAT WAS DAVE DOING WRONG?

While Dave was using a good healthy variety of different types and levels of questions, the problem was that all of his questions were either *dangling* or *anonymous*. With a dangling question, the teacher addresses no one in particular. The teacher asks the question, as Dave did (such as, "Which area gets the least amount of rain?"), and it dangles there in the air waiting for someone to respond. That is the problem. Students *do* respond. They respond with no sense of order or respect for others. Those who are so inclined simply yell out their answers. Why do they do this? They do this because there is no direction from the teacher. The teacher has asked an undirected question and this results in disorganized, scattered, and loud responses usually from a handful of students.

STUDENTS LEFT IN THE DARK

It is not only the yelling out that is the problem. Very often, the teacher hears the "right" answer from among the responses the students yell, grabs onto that answer (without necessarily repeating the response), and praises the student(s) and moves on. But much of the class is left with no idea which of the yelled out answers was the appropriate one. Students cannot discriminate the way the teacher can. They are often in back of or to the side of the students who yell out and cannot even hear the response; on the other hand, the teacher is most often facing the students and can hear these yelled out answers. If students can't hear, they won't and can't be engaged.

WORSE CONSEQUENCES

Much worse for classroom management than students not hearing is what the yelling out leads to very quickly in the class. Here is what happens to the classroom dynamic:

1. The same four or five students, who are usually the loudest, quickest, and most aggressive students, continue to yell out answers to other questions.

2. The quieter and less confident students withdraw. They can't respond as quickly as those who yell out and, feeling abandoned, either they stop making attempts to respond or start to act out in class or both.

3. The students who don't respond are left unclear as to what the answer might be and are too intimidated or too disinterested to ask.

4. Worse, the teacher is, in effect, working with a class of four or five students. That is where the teacher directs his attention, most often because he feels safe with those few students or because he is simply unaware of what he is doing.

5. Those four or five students realize very quickly that they have gotten control of both the classroom and the teacher and they run with the power; the classroom deteriorates.

6. Some teachers may recognize the inequity among students in the situation and not know what to do; the classroom continues to deteriorate.

7. Some teachers concentrate so hard on these few students and are so happy that the students are providing answers that they don't even notice the lack of

participation by the majority of the class or that anything else is askew in the class; the classroom continues
to deteriorate.

8. Some teachers may recognize that only a few are participating but may be too intimidated to call on other
students for fear those students may not know the
answer or may respond in a disrespectful way, and consequently will disrupt the class even further; the classroom continues to deteriorate.

9. Some teachers believe the class is overrun with "awful
kids"; that is, those kids who are not paying attention,
those kids who are poking and disturbing others, those
kids who don't participate.

In reality, the teacher is responsible for, has caused, and
continues to perpetuate this lopsided, loud, threatening,
unsafe, and ineffective dynamic which disrupts and usually
prevents any kind of real learning or sense of belonging for
the majority of students.

What Can You Do?

To avoid or fix this destructive dynamic, you will need to
explain to the class that you are henceforth going to have a
new policy in the room. You will call on a student by name
and only that person will respond. You may be tempted to try
another solution; i.e., you may tell students to raise their
hands and you will call on a student in that way.

The Problems With Hand Raising

There are problems, though, with hand raising. It is almost
always those same students who yell out so quickly, eagerly,
and aggressively who raise their hands first. Some even shake
an arm around and yell, "Oh, oh, oh!" Student and novice

teachers, especially, but also many experienced teachers, respond to those first-raised hands and the results are the same cockeyed power in the hands of a few, the same lack of positive student involvement, and the same disruption in the classroom.

Some teachers do learn to wait for more students to raise their hands, but in the long run, seeing hands raised is just as disconcerting as yelled out answers to those students who aren't confident enough or quick enough to respond. It takes a skilled teacher and lots of practice to be able to calm down the quick hand raisers without defusing their interest and at the same time to involve the rest of the students equally, even when they are not raising their hands. If you ask students to raise their hands to answer, and then you call on students who are not raising their hands in an attempt to get them involved, the class gets very confused as to why you are asking them to raise their hands in the first place.

If your class is already in disarray, this process is only going to confuse them more. Stick to calling students by name until the class is back under control and you are feeling secure and the students are feeling safe. If you are a new teacher or it is the beginning of your practicum or the beginning of the school year, calling students by name will give everyone—you and the students—a sense of order in the classroom. Once the classroom has become a strong, interactive, and involved community of learners, you can try other approaches.

A BETTER WAY

A better way to ask questions and at the same time create a safe and totally involved class is to:

1. Ask students to write down, on paper or on a white board, their response to the question (or for very young children, to draw their response).

2. Give them an appropriate time to do it.

3. Call on students by name.

Explain that this is what you will do. This process allows all students time to think and doesn't relinquish leadership of the class to the four or five quickest and loudest students.

Having students work in pairs gives students even more confidence to answer. (Working in pairs can be more problematic for some classes than others. If it won't work with your class(es), stick to having students write down their answers before calling on anyone.) Working on the question with a peer allows a student to feel less vulnerable when answering. As a bonus, the process of students working in pairs encourages the development of student-to-student interaction and the beginning, or enhancement, of classroom connections.

An Old Teacher's (or Is It a Researcher's?) Tale

There is an old teacher's tale out there in education land that suggests you should not use a student's name *before* you ask a question, but at the end of the question. The reasoning is that if you use a particular student's name at the beginning, the rest of the class will drift or just plain zone out. *Pay no attention to this.* If you ask the question first and then use a student's name, already it will be too late. Those same aggressive and fast students will be yelling out before you get to the name. Use the student's name first, but remind students ahead of time that you will be calling on more than one person. This will keep all involved mentally. When you call on the second student, say something like, "Zach, how would you answer the same question?" or "Michelle, what can you add to that response?" This improves student attention and the students get to hear two, possibly different, responses which can lead to discussion and more learning.

The Results of These Better Strategies

Not only do these strategies prevent classroom chaos, they allow everyone to be equally involved; they allow you to be in control; they allow those who need longer to process the question and response, the time they need without feeling slow or incompetent or inferior; and they force the fast responders to spend more time thinking. Everyone wins. Everyone can feel like and become a valuable part of the class.

Anonymous Questions: What Are They?

What results in your class from the use of *anonymous* questions (and Dave was using plenty of these as well) will be exactly the same as the results you get when you use dangling questions: a handful of students yelling out and controlling the classroom; other students withdrawing, feeling unsafe and less able; students not paying attention; some students feeling ignored and misbehaving; a classroom in disarray; and a lack of learning. Here is what anonymous questions sound like:

1. "*Who* can tell me the capital of Virginia?"

2. "Is *everyone* ready?" (What was Dave's question about the homework?)

3. "Does *anyone* know why leaves change color?"

4. "Can *someone* explain the causes of the French Revolution?"

5. "Do you *all* understand the directions?"

6. "Can *anyone* define anonymous and dangling questions?"

What's Wrong With *These* Questions?

They are anonymous. No one in your class knows to whom you are speaking. Should they respond? Shouldn't they respond? They don't know what they are supposed to do. No one in your class is named "Who," or "Everyone," or "Anyone," or "Someone," or "All." The students need more direction from you. The use of anonymous pronouns leads invariably to the same chaotic, unfocused, misbehaving classroom as does the use of dangling questions.

How Can A Teacher Fix This?

Questions 1, 3, and 4

In the same way teachers should use students' names to avoid the repercussions of using dangling questions, they should use students' names instead of anonymous pronouns. You can change questions 1, 3, and 4 above by using a student's name:

1. "Shelly, what is the capital of Virginia?"

3. "John, please explain to the class why leaves change color."

4. "Koushek, please review one major cause of the French Revolution."

To avoid other students from disconnecting when you call on a particular person, remind them that you will ask more than one person to either respond or add to the original response. Explain why you are doing this.

What About Question 2?

Question 2 ("Is everyone ready?") is not only an anonymous question, it provides you with no kind of useful information; it leads to misunderstandings between you and your students; and it directly causes disruptions as students begin a task and reveal quickly that they weren't ready when you asked, or didn't understand the directions, even though they didn't let you know. The few students who nod their heads or yell out "yes" fool you into thinking "everyone" is ready. When Dave heard the two or three students answer "yes" to his question, "Did everyone complete the homework?" he made the mistake of thinking all of the students had completed the homework and were ready for his questions.

It was a faulty assumption. Not all of his students had completed the homework. When you ask questions like "Is everybody ready" or "Did everyone complete the homework?" none of the students know how to respond. Some may yell out "yes." Others will be silent. You may hear "yes" and move on. Disaster follows and you can't figure out why. To ensure that students are ready or that all students did their homework, you have to check in with every student. In Dave's case, he should have checked everyone's homework before beginning.

Question 5

"Do you all understand the directions?" is an anonymous question that like question 2 provides no useful information and leads to student confusion and many class disruptions. It is important for teachers to know that students understand directions before allowing the class to begin a task. Without assuring that every student is ready and understands, there will be disruptions and distractions throughout the class or time period as students have to ask for meaning or a repeat of explanations that you thought were clear. A few students answering "yes" does not mean that all students understand the directions or instructions. Chapter 4 will explain what to do to insure students are ready and do understand directions before they begin a particular task.

Before we jump that far ahead, what happened to Dave?

DID DAVE RECOVER?

Dave wasn't buying my theory that his lack of direction and his use of dangling and anonymous questions were causing or encouraging the student misbehavior. He declared he had never heard of dangling or anonymous questions anyway. No wonder. The terms are not in the literature. Well, they are now. I developed this nomenclature after many years of observing the same phenomenon and issues. Just as many student teachers do, Dave believed students would think he was picking on them if he called them by name and that it would stunt students' freedom and individuality. (Students often do feel picked on until the teacher explains the purpose and rationale of calling on them by name. Having students work in pairs can eliminate this issue.) Dave believed it was much more beneficial and liberating for students to make their own decisions as to when and if they would respond to questions.

THE EXPERIMENT

Dave did, however, agree to an experiment. For the next week, Dave continued to do what he had been doing and video-taped his class every day. At the end of that week, we viewed the tapes together. Very little had changed except that maybe the class behavior had deteriorated further. Dave remarked at how exhausted he looked in the video.

For the following week, Dave agreed to videotape his class daily again, but this time he would try making changes. He would try to avoid dangling and anonymous questions; he would have students work in pairs and would have them write down their responses; he would preface each question with a particular student's name; and he would ask more than one student about the same question. He also agreed to explain to the class what he was going to do and why he was making changes.

THE RESULTS

At the end of the week, Dave and I met and he reluctantly confessed that he was feeling safer and more in control;

he also felt that the students were participating more, were more engaged, and were behaving better. Then we reviewed the tapes together. I was not surprised at the results. Dave was shocked. He was astounded at just how different his class had become. He didn't particularly like admitting that the changes were not only helping, but that everything in his class had improved—student attention, student learning, student behavior, student respect, and his confidence. This week, they weren't such "awful kids," and Dave didn't look so tired.

Dave continued to improve in his ability to develop, pose, and direct questions in a way that encouraged positive student behavior, engagement, and higher level learning while maintaining, at the same time, a safe classroom decorum. His confidence continued to grow as did the students' respect for him. His practicum was a great success. The following year, Dave became a teacher in a different school system and two years later he became the mentor for new teachers in the system.

SUMMARY: STEP 2

1. Avoid dangling questions (questions that hang in the air).

2. Avoid anonymous questions (questions that use anonymous pronouns such as "anyone," "someone," "everybody," "all," "who").

3. Instead:

    Explain to students that you will be calling on at least two students, then call on the first student by name and ask the question. Call on a second student by name and ask the student to expand or clarify.

    Give students, either as individuals or in pairs, appropriate time to write down answers (or to draw answers if students are younger) and then call on specific students to give answers or show their drawings.

What's Next?

Chapter 3 examines word use and explains how important language is to classroom management. The chapter looks at how unnecessary filler and unprofessional words can lead to disorder and disruption and, conversely, how civil and positive language can help to create a safe, orderly, calm, and respectful classroom environment. This is probably the easiest of the Six Simple Steps, but can have a huge impact on student behavior and civility in the classroom.

3

Choosing and Using Words Wisely

MARIAH

The Context

Mariah had been teaching language arts for almost 20 years when the state in which she was teaching mandated that all teachers in Grades 5 through 8 earn middle school certification. Mariah had a secondary school teaching certificate that applied to Grades 7 through 12, and even though she was and had been teaching in Grade 8, she was required to earn the new middle school certification or forfeit her position to a new teacher who did.

She was one of 36 teachers at her school who joined the Middle School Curriculum and Instruction class (a state-required course) that I was teaching on-site. As part of this class, the teachers would implement a series of new learning plans in alignment with the new certification requirements, which focused on student-centered learning processes, rather than teacher-centered teaching processes.

The School

Mariah's Grade 5 through 8 middle school was located in a small, upper socioeconomic suburb (population approximately 3600) of a small city in a state known for its progressive thinking. The student population was about 98 percent White and 2 percent Asian and American Indian. The school had been built in the 1960s and showcased the open classroom architecture popular at the time. All classrooms were open to the circular main corridor and also to the central library beyond the corridor. No classroom had more than three walls. From a classroom management viewpoint, the structure of the school was a nightmare, with sounds from all the rooms, the corridor, and the library reverberating around like erratic flying saucers. Students in the back of each classroom tended to be hopelessly distracted by what was happening in the corridor and the library. It took a very strong teacher with very engaging lessons to keep the students focused.

MARIAH'S GOAL

Mariah's goal in terms of her new certification was to change her teaching from a stand and deliver approach to one in which the students would participate in developing and implementing the curriculum using a process developed by James Beane (1997). I observed her class as she taught in her familiar format so that we could discuss an appropriate starting point for her new efforts. For a review on the unit on writing and grammar, Mariah had paragraphs on newsprint hung from the top ridges of the whiteboard and was pointing to and asking questions about the grammar issues in each of the paragraphs. She called on students by name, involved all the students, and avoided using dangling and anonymous questions. Those were the pluses.

The Problem

"This sentence, um, is somewhat, um, like the last. Zack, um, do you know, um, why?"

"There are, um, two, um, mistakes in the, um, next, um, paragraph. Sarah, what, um, are they?"

Students began to mentally wander fairly quickly. "Guys, listen up," Mariah ordered as she saw and felt their waning interest. "This is really important, right?"

It is not easy to engage students in a lesson on grammar, but Mariah was making it much more difficult for students to stay on task by using filler words that cut up her thoughts and her sentences and slowed her already slow pace even more. As I watched and listened to Mariah, I was struck by how nearly impossible it was for me, never mind the eighth graders, to stay focused on what she was saying.

Yawning and More

Mariah continued in the same way, using multiple filler words and then repeating, "Guys, listen up," as students drifted. Most of the students were not misbehaving overtly, just looking bored and disconnected; some were yawning. However, there were three young men who started to talk among themselves. Then they began to make sounds and poke each other every time Mariah turned away from them. Mariah gave them all afternoon detentions for their transgressions. Actually, I felt it was a good sign they were talking and moving, because Mariah's language could easily have induced comas, which would have been much worse. What did Mariah have to do, what *could* she do, to get her class back?

WHAT'S IN A WORD?

What's in a word? In the world of research or literature on classroom management, apparently not much. You can find research and writing on how important it is to know the meaning of students' slang in urban and multicultural settings so as to not seem or look intimidated by students (Foster, 1986); or on how to manage inappropriate student language such as cursing in the classroom (Jay, 1996). You can even find articles or research on the negative consequences of teacher language that humiliates or shames students (Zeidner, 1988).

But this chapter is about how *your* language can impact your classroom environment, which in turn affects how students behave (Jones & Jones, 2004). Language *does* matter in classroom management and the first half of this chapter focuses on teacher unprofessional, sloppy, tedious, monotonous, or unnecessary language and how it negatively impacts student behavior and engagement.

THE IMPORTANCE OF TIGHT AND PROFESSIONAL LANGUAGE

George Orwell

George Orwell (1946) believed that correct speech allows people to think more clearly:

> [. . .] the slovenliness of our language makes it easier for us to have foolish thoughts [. . .] Modern English, especially written English, is full of bad habits which spread by imitation and which can be avoided if one is willing to take the necessary trouble. If one gets rid of these habits one can think more clearly [. . .] so that the fight against bad English is not frivolous and is not the exclusive concern of professional writers. (par. 2)

Sloppy Language

George Orwell may or may not have been right, but it is clear, from monitoring hundreds of preservice teachers as they conducted lessons in their methods courses, from watching over 1500 videotapes of student teachers, and from working with over 500 inservice teachers, that sloppy and unprofessional speech on the part of teachers is not only rampant, but it can lead to all kinds of trouble.

WHAT ARE FILLER WORDS?

Have you, uh, ever tried to, uh, listen, uh, to a person, um, who keeps using, um, filler words? Words that are unnecessary, have no meaning, and interrupt the flow of your sentences and speaking are filler words. There are many. Two of the most common filler words (or utterances) are "uh" and, Mariah's favorite, "um." But there are many others. Here are some common examples:

1. "The first part, *OK*, of the project, *OK*, will be to do research, *OK*, and then, *OK*, we will come back to class, *OK?*"

It's the overuse of and lack of meaning in this word that makes it a filler word. I have heard some student teachers and new teachers use this almost every time they take a breath. It's a sure sign to their students that they are anxious, intimidated, tired, unsure, indifferent, or unprepared.

2. "*Like*, we are going on a field trip, *like*, tomorrow. If we have time, *like*, we will, *like*, review items today."

Just about the only thing the word "like" means in these sentences is that the teacher is not focused on the thoughts and words.

3. "Napoleon, *right*, had to consider all his options, *right?*"

4. "We are going, *right*, to conduct research, *right*, on volcanoes, *right?*"

5. "It is important, *right*, to use apostrophes in the right place, *right?*"

You get the idea. I doubt any teacher would write using filler words. Why would the same teacher, then, speak using them?

What Happens When You Use Filler Words?

Boredom and Worse

Filler words, as Mariah was using, not only make for inter-rupted speech and thought but also for bored students, the last thing you want. It creates the perfect environment for devilment. But, there is more to this kind of speech than that it is boring. Language interrupted and laced with filler words sends the message to students that you are not really inter-ested in what you are saying, don't really know what you are talking about, simply have no energy, or don't care enough about the students to make more effort on their behalf.

A Mirror Image

Your energy, interest, and passion are reflected back to you by your students. If you are, or appear to be, bored; or don't, or appear to not, care about what you are doing or teaching; or you have, or appear to have, little energy or passion for what you are doing, that is what your students will bounce back at you in their behaviors. A boring, disinterested, or de-energized classroom is not conducive to learning; it is a breeding ground for disorder and mayhem. Filler words affect the pace of your speech dramatically. That, in turn, impacts the energy and tempo in the classroom, leads to lack of student attention, and to students using what energy they have in unproductive and disruptive ways.

An Unprofessional Word

Besides eliminating the filler words, there was something else Mariah needed to change. It involved a problem common among teachers and that is the use of nonprofessional lan-guage that weakens the teacher's leadership position in the classroom and blurs the boundaries that need to be in place to ensure a safe and nondisruptive classroom for all the students. Included in many teachers' unprofessional language is one word that is so prevalent as to make one's hair curl (or straighten, as the case may be). It seems like such a harmless word. It is used everywhere, with friends, at home, at work, in meetings, on TV, and in the movies. Mariah used it often. Can you guess what it is?

A Test

Here are some questions with a missing word:

1. "Will you _____ please get into groups and continue to work on yesterday's project?"

2. "Good Morning, _____. Today you _____ will learn how to set up science experiments."

3. "OK, _____, you have 15 minutes left to finish that problem."

4. "_____, please prepare to speak in front of the class."

5. "You _____ have done a terrific job."

The Answer

What is the word that is missing? . . . Actually, there is no word missing or necessary in those blanks. Remove the blanks and you have complete, direct, clear sentences. That is what you need to remember most; no word is missing or necessary there. While you may think this is no big deal as far as the maintaining of our English language, in terms of classroom management and professionalism, what this word does is take the respectful and professional teacher-student relationship and turn it into a chummy kind of connection with unclear boundaries.

You also may think that acting like a chum is endearing to your students. It is not. It is clear from hundreds of student evaluations of teachers that the one thing they need, want, and expect is a teacher who is the leader and who ensures a safe, nondisruptive classroom for them. You are not their peer. They don't want you as a peer. You are their leader. But if you don't speak and act like a leader, students will not treat you like the leader; classroom decorum will suffer and, without a strong and effective leader, students feel less safe and act up more.

Hey, guys, have you figured it out yet? *Guys!* The word is "guys." If you are guilty, try speaking without any word where you would normally use "guys." There is no context in which this word is professional or necessary. If you feel it is absolutely necessary to put in some kind of word in those blanks, there are other words you can use that are professional and lead to a different response from the students. Teacher recommendations, which may seem old fashioned, but have positive and behavior changing results, are: "class," "folks," and "ladies and gentlemen." Teaching is a lot about trial and error. You have nothing to lose by trying these other words. You have nothing to lose by eliminating the word "guys," except the word "guys." And you have everything to gain by using more professional language.

MARIAH'S TRANSFORMATION

Mariah was brave enough and cooperative enough to agree to videotape her class for the next few days. When she watched and listened to herself on the tape, she was surprised and appalled at how weak and disjointed she sounded, and she agreed that she, too, would be bored or into trouble if she were a student in her own class. Before we could launch into a new teaching and learning approach, Mariah had to pick up her pace, omit the filler words, and replace "Guys, listen up" with more professional language. There wasn't much point in taking these detrimental behaviors and speech into a new approach; they would undermine the effectiveness of the new plans.

Mariah wasn't sure this was going to work, but decided, as a prelude to the new middle school requirements of a learner-centered approach, to involve the students in helping her change her speech. Every time she used a filler word or "guys" or "listen up," the students held up rulers. It became quite a game and not only was it successful, it demonstrated how much more engaged students are when they have a say in the class. By the end of the week, Mariah's language, pace, and student focus had improved.

THE RESULTS

Mariah continued to work on her language as she transitioned into her new plans. The students were playing a greater role in developing and conducting the class and part of their learning had to do with avoiding filler and unprofessional language when they spoke in class. Everyone benefited from the new language in terms of focus, learning, pace, lack of boredom, and, if George Orwell was correct, from improved thought patterns.

THE OTHER SIDE OF THE LANGUAGE COIN

Now that we have examined some of the words to omit from your teaching, let's focus on the other part of Step 3—on how to embed and teach words of civility in classroom communication and activity, and how doing so can help to change the classroom dynamic and develop a safe environment less prone to lack of respect, disorder, and disruption, and more conducive to learning. Consider the following scenarios.

TERRY

The Context

Terry was in his first year of teaching fifth-grade math at a middle school in an ethnically and racially diverse city with a population of about 300,000. There were notes about double the size of a postcard taped to all the outside doors of the school that welcomed students, teachers, and visitors:

> **Anyone found carrying a gun to school will be suspended for one week.**

It was an old school in what 20 years before had been a safe and higher socioeconomic area of the city. Now it was a transitional neighborhood that had a reputation of being a high crime area. Because of prior trouble in the school, all of the bathrooms were locked except for one boy's and one girl's bathroom; the teachers took turns sitting outside of each of those bathrooms to check student passes. The corridors were noisy and raucous; the classes averaged 35 students.

The Problem

Terry learned very quickly how difficult it can be to teach in an inner-city school, especially with students who speak little or no English. The newest immigrants to the city and his class were from Russia and Pakistan. Their command of the English language ranged from none to mediocre. The upside for Terry was that numbers are universal and he was able to have some success in visually explaining arithmetic operations to most of the students. But he was feeling overwhelmed as he struggled to teach not only with the language difficulties but amid a general lack of civility and different cultural norms. Some students seemed to have no idea of how to behave in a classroom or among other people. Some got out of their seats and roamed around whenever they wanted; some had much difficulty focusing on anything; some responded in negative tones in a foreign language. What did Terry need to do? What could he do?

AND DANAE

The Context

Danae, a student teacher, was very happy to learn that she would be teaching the advanced placement (AP) classes in

Spanish at a prominent high school in an affluent town next to a prestigious university. She believed the students would be too focused on academics to give her much trouble.

It was a small high school of approximately 400 students—about 85 percent White, 14 percent Asian and Indian, and 1 percent Black and Latino. The teachers and students considered this an academic high school to such a degree that they declared with an unusual pride that there was no football team at the school, as if having a football team would somehow dilute the academic accomplishments and reputation.

The Problem

While most of the students in her AP class were attentive to Danae, there were two young men who constantly interrupted her and other students with their antics. If they weren't talking or slipping notes to each other, they were snickering under their breath at what other students or Danae was saying. Danae was in a kind of shock because she had made the assumption before she began her practicum that students in AP classes at a prestigious school would not disrupt her classes, that AP students never disrupted classes.

She had only three weeks left in the practicum when her anxiety over the behavior of the two young men reached monumental proportions. She had tried several approaches to solving the problem including moving their seats (this rarely works, because it doesn't address the real issue), talking to the young men before class, talking to them during class, talking to them after class, giving them detentions, and threatening them with a trip to the principal's office. All of her actions were met with behind-her-back snickering, more disruptions, and more inventive mischief from the two young men. They knew they were rattling her; to them it was a game. Danae felt like a failure and didn't understand why they didn't "like" her. Outside of the class, she was often in tears. She was becoming physically ill thinking about going into the class each day. What could Danae do?

Using Words of Civility in the Classroom

The basic steps of classroom management are really very simple. What happens if you don't know about these steps and don't use these steps is not simple. You will undermine your own hard work, and classroom disorder will lead to exhaustion, crying, hiding in the teacher's lounge, vomiting (as with Danae), and even quitting.

Given that students want and need a safe environment and react positively to such a culture (Alder & Moulton, 1998; Cothran, Kilinna, & Garrahy, 2003; Supaporn, 2000), one of the simplest ways to use language in the classroom to create that safe culture is to teach civility through your own behavior and language—the same way that Mariah was teaching better speech patterns by using better speech patterns.

Five Important Words

There are three words (or forms of these words) that are critical in creating a civil environment and that should always be on the tip of your tongue. The words are *cooperate, appreciate,* and *appropriate.* If you put these words together with *thank you* and *please,* you make it difficult for students to misbehave. You speak to them with respect and it is more likely that they will mirror the behavior than not.

Examples

Consider these examples and visualize a quiet and calm tone:

1. "Class, we are going to review yesterday's problems. I *appreciate* your complete attention. *Thank you.*"

2. "Before we move to the library, *please* assemble the necessary papers. I *appreciate* your *cooperation. Thank you.*"

3. "Linda, I need you to *cooperate, please . . . ;* (delay slightly, then) *thank you.*"

4. "Julien, I would *appreciate* it if you would pay attention to Sam . . . ; (delay slightly) *thank you.*"

5. "Alia, *please* use *appropriate* language and *please* focus on the work . . . ; *thank you; I appreciate* it."

It is so simple to move your class in the direction of civility. It just takes practice and some concentration until using this language becomes automatic. Since not all students have experience with these words (and this can be especially true of minority and disadvantaged students [Banks & Banks, 2004]), for diverse classrooms, in particular, your explanations about language in your classroom are very important.

But what was it that Terry and Danae had in common, how was it connected to classroom language and civility, and how did they mend their classes?

THE COMMON THREAD

Terry and Danae had very different classes and were in very different schools in different parts of the country. One thing they had in common, however, was the need for their students to learn a common language and behavior of civility.

Terry

Terry was overwhelmed. He not only had to deal with language barriers but also students who were being disruptive, misbehaving, not attending to the task, being rude, and being disrespectful to other students and to him. He had to begin with the basics. Without the grounding and requirements or student understanding of simple and civil behavior, he couldn't make any headway. His teacher preparation program had not prepared him for this.

Most of Terry's students (as Banks and Banks [2004] found among minority or disadvantaged students), including those who did speak English, had had little experience with the words "thank you," and "please," so his math class had to first become a class in language. He asked Kachina, the English Second Language (ESL) teacher to come into his room and work with all of his students to help them learn the meaning and use of "please" and "thank you" as well as of the three other important words: "appreciate," "cooperate," and "appropriate."

Kachina practiced the words with the students. First she modeled when to say "thank you" by having the students open the door for her and then responding, "Thank you." Then she did the reverse—she opened the door for them so that they could practice "thank you." She used several other scenarios including handing out papers and accepting things from students. In similar kinds of modeling, she taught them when to use "please." Teaching the meanings of "appreciate," "cooperate," and "appropriate" wasn't quite as easy, but Kachina did it, again with a lot of modeling and even showing video clips of word-defining actions.

Although Terry's class continued to be a challenge, once the students grasped, at least at some level, these words, it was easier for Terry to use words to prevent and handle the interruptions in the class. He and the students continued to practice the words in relation to behavior in every context of their class and Kachina continued to help develop the students' understanding of critically important words of civility.

Danae

As with many student and new teachers, Danae had waited too long to think about, introduce, use, and require words and behavior of civility. She had made the faulty assumption before she began her practicum that students in AP classes are never disruptive.

What Danae learned was that all students are capable of playing pranks, of being rude, and of creating mayhem. And it didn't take much to do that—a mumbled word here, a facial expression there, hand signals anywhere. Because these two young men had behaved inappropriately for so long, her attempts at changing their behaviors weren't having much effect. She had little credibility with them because, although she spoke to them often about their behavior, she didn't really have any force or follow through behind her words. They continued to misbehave and interrupt class.

Danae had to start over from the beginning and to do that, she had to send the young men to spend two days of quality time with the mentor teacher in another classroom. Once the young men realized their antics were not going to work anymore, they settled down. Danae was then able, even at that late stage in the practicum, to talk to the class about civil language and civil behavior, and what her expectations were of the students. She spent the last three weeks of her practicum implementing and practicing the new civil language requirements with her class. "Please" and "thank you" became a daily part of the classroom language. Just having "appreciate," "cooperate," and "appropriate" on the tip of her tongue made Danae more confident. She was no longer fumbling around trying to figure out what to say to keep her class calm, to prevent unwanted disruptions, and to refocus student attention. It is never too late to teach and learn about civility.

THREE OTHER POWERFUL HINTS ABOUT LANGUAGE

Besides these important words of civility, there are three other suggestions about language that belong here and that can help eliminate a disruptive environment while establishing a productive and safe learning environment.

1. Language Tone: You Don't Need to Yell

If you are yelling, something is wrong with your classroom management approach. Yelling at students is rarely effective in getting their attention or reducing disruption or unwanted behavior. It may make a difference or put a stop to something for the moment, but it won't carry over to or prevent other situations, other behaviors, or incidences. And, it is not only not necessary, it models an unfortunate example for the students, upsets them, jars the classroom, and often leads to resistance, antagonism, lack of cooperation, and worse behavior. What can you do instead? Implement the Six Simple Steps in this book.

2. The Power of No Language

Do you get rattled just trying to get your class's attention? Do you assume, as Barry did, that the students will stop talking if you just start? This is a very bad mistake. Not only do you look unaware, incompetent, and frightened when you do this, but you also lose valuable learning time as the students have to ask over and over, "What did you say?" "What are we supposed to do?"

One of the simplest ways to get the attention of a class is to stand in front of the class silently while making eye contact with one, then another, then another student. Students will spread the word very quickly and quietly that they need to be silent and pay attention. Usually in less than twenty seconds, the entire class will be silent and focused on you. If it takes longer than this, simply call on one or two students who are still talking and say something like, "Sarah, please . . . I am waiting for you. (pause) Thank you."

3. Getting the Class's Attention While They Are Involved in Group Work

Students can get very involved when they are working in groups, which is, of course, what you want. But trying to get their attention for an announcement or to bring them back to a whole class format can lead some teachers to yell louder and louder. If the students are on task and highly engaged in their work with other students, yelling at them will only aggravate them and make you hoarse and tired. There is a very simple alternative. Start going to one group at a time and very quietly say, "I need you to be *silent* now, we are going to come together again as a class. Thank you." Go to the next group and repeat the same. You will have to go to only one or two groups. The others will hear the silence from other parts of the room and will stop talking and focus on you.

The Power of Silence

There is a big difference between using the word "silence" and using the word "quiet." If you want silence, you have to use that word (or "silent," depending on the sentence). There is no misinterpretation of that word. But there is much misinterpretation of the word "quiet." To some students, it means whisper; to others, it means talk softly; to other students, it means nothing at all—they think they are already being quiet. You can't blame students if you ask them to be quiet and they continue to talk. Use the word you mean.

MAKING THESE LANGUAGE AND TONE CHANGES IN YOUR CLASSROOM

If you are a preservice teacher and are able to practice these language changes when you conduct a college methods class or in your practicum, they will become second nature to you; you will be prepared as you enter the real world of teaching. If you are a novice or experienced teacher, you have the perfect audience to assist in these changes. The easiest way to eliminate filler words, to add words of civility, and to avoid yelling is to explain to the students why you want to make the changes and then ask for their help in monitoring you. Students of all ages love to do this and as a complementary benefit, the students themselves start to use these professional and civil words and language. Even better, it is a way to promote a sense of community in your classroom.

SUMMARY: STEP 3

1. Eliminate filler words like "uh," "OK," and "right."

2. Eliminate the use of "guys." Replace with words like "folks," "class," and "ladies and gentlemen."

3. Use the words (and forms of these words) "cooperate," "appreciate," and "appropriate" whenever possible.

4. "Thank you" and "please" go a long way to creating civility.

5. To get a class's attention, stand quietly in front of the class and make eye contact with one student after another until everyone is silent.

6. To get the attention of students involved in group work, go to one group at a time and request their silence.

COMING ATTRACTIONS

Steps 1, 2, and 3 (knowing and using the students' names; addressing a particular student to avoid dangling and anonymous questions; and avoiding sloppy and unprofessional speech while adding in words of civility) provide basic grounding, organization, and preparation for a chaos-free classroom. Steps 4, 5, and 6 will continue to examine ways to establish a safe and positive climate while at the same time creating a productive classroom characterized by on-task and highly engaged students. Chapter 4 focuses on how to avoid confusion when giving directions and consequently how to have fewer disruptions, more engaged students, and more learning.

4

Avoiding Confusion When Giving Directions

ELIZABETH

Class Begins

As the sixth graders pushed and shoved their way into the classroom, they paid no attention to Elizabeth, who had been their student teacher in world geography for the last two months. Elizabeth was leaning over her podium shuffling papers, looking blank, and seemingly oblivious to the tripping, smacking, and other typically middle school behaviors that were happening in the doorways and leading into the room.

Two young men walked up one aisle, one jabbing the other in the ribs, saw the video camera at the back of the room that was ready to tape the class, and proceeded to make all kinds of faces up against the camera lens. One of them pulled his cheeks as far apart as he could, stuck his tongue out, and crossed his eyes. It is an image forever captured on the tape.

The bell rang and Elizabeth repeated five or six times: "Listen up." She waited each time for the class's attention. It came only after Elizabeth suddenly and loudly whacked her ruler on the podium.

The Context

Elizabeth's practicum was in a mostly (94 percent) White middle school in a working-class city of about 34,000, located outside of a large metropolitan area. Elizabeth's mentor teacher was of little help. He was the football coach at the local high school and, after teaching his morning classes in the middle school, he often would head over to the high school, basically abandoning Elizabeth and leaving her in charge of the classes she was assigned to teach. A conversation with the mentor and the principal did little to alleviate that problem, but Elizabeth insisted that she wanted to continue in that placement rather than move to another (a mistake I didn't make twice). Elizabeth did not look happy; she rarely smiled; she did not look confident; she did not look in control, and she seemed to have little energy. She looked like she wanted to run away.

The day's class consisted of a review of geography terms. Elizabeth had decided to do this review in a game format, something I would not recommend for student teachers because such formats require a high level of skill at managing.

Her Instructions

"Today we are going to review the geography terms we have been studying. There will be two teams. This side of the room [she motioned to the right] will be Team A. This side of the room [she motioned to the left] will be Team B. Each time I ask a question, one person from each team will come to the board and write the answer. The first person to write the correct answer gets one point for their team. Your turns will be in order of your seats, so Jack from Team A and Jen from

Team B will be the first; next will be whoever sits behind them and so on. Here is the first question."

Pandemonium

"What is a low, watery land formed at the mouth of a river?"

Jack and Jen jumped up at approximately the same time. Jack pushed Jen back, raced up to the board and wrote "delta."

"One point for Team A," Elizabeth declared as she made a vertical mark under the Team A name at the side of the board. She didn't mention that Jack had pushed Jen or, in fact, that there were any special behavior considerations to this game. Team A started screaming and pounding their fists on their desks.

"What is a river of ice?"

Lauren, on Team A, struggled to move, and it was obvious from her grimaces that she didn't know the answer. Beth, from Team B, ran to the board and wrote "glaser." Lauren never did bother to get up.

"One point for Team B." Now it was Team B's turn to raise a ruckus and they did. This time it was stomping of feet and shouting an extended, "Yea!" Once again, there was no response from Elizabeth. She didn't even correct the spelling.

She continued, "What is a narrow strip of land that connects two large land masses?"

Craig from Team A jumped up, turned his desk and chair over to block Sean from Team B and ran to the board. Sean bounded down a different aisle. Somehow they got to the board at about the same time. Craig wrote, "Who cares?" in very large letters. Sean took the chalk and, in sweeping round movements, made about 10 circles on the board.

Elizabeth meekly told the class, "No more drawing on the board; you can only write answers," and continued on.

The class was out of control. I had my own dilemma: Should I stop the class myself before someone got injured, or should I let it continue to give Elizabeth the chance to stop the class herself, recoup, and do something different? I chose, in retrospect perhaps wrongly, to let it continue. And it did. The noise got louder and louder. A teacher from the next room opened the adjoining door, yelled, "Quiet down in there," and in retreat slammed the door with a vengeance.

CLARIFYING DIRECTIONS

Besides knowing and using the students' names every time you speak to them, besides avoiding anonymous and dangling questions, and besides retooling your language and tone in class, there is almost nothing more important to insuring a smoothly running, disruption-free class than giving clear directions and making sure that students understand those directions. In Elizabeth's case, she did give directions, but there was no checking for student understanding. Could others help with the answers? Was there a time limit? If the person whose turn it was didn't know the answer, could someone else take his place? What if both students wrote incorrect answers? What if there was a tie at the board?

And, Elizabeth failed to explain behavior parameters. Was it acceptable to run? Could you look in the book for the answer? Could you write an answer on a piece of paper and give it to the person who needed to answer? Could you block other students?

Did Elizabeth recover from this calamity?

THE RESULTS

Elizabeth was lost; the class was a disaster. Luckily no one did get hurt, and finally, after what seemed like forever, the bell mercifully rang. The students practically threw themselves out of the room. Following the class, Elizabeth and I had a conference in which my main question to her was, "What worked and what didn't?" There was almost no awareness on her part of what had happened in the class. She did think the students were too noisy, but other than that, she thought it went "OK."

We then reviewed the tape and discussed where things needed to be improved. We talked at length about how to give directions and instructions that would prevent disruptions, but Elizabeth seemed less than inventive with her own ideas and less than receptive to mine. There were many other things wrong with Elizabeth's lesson plan. For example, you don't want to have students writing answers on the board if, for whatever reason, they are poor spellers. It is humiliating for students to have to showcase their weaknesses to their peers. Rather than appear stupid, often students will act silly and lapse into nonsensical behavior as Sean did when he drew the circles. Verbal responses would have worked better, as would have working in pairs. But no game format works well if the instructions are not crystal clear in terms of both the game rules and the behavior limits. Along with this, the teacher must also check for student understanding.

Elizabeth did finish out the practicum, but decided that teaching was not the career for her. She went on to graduate school to study business. I, on the other hand, had to own the responsibility for my lack of proactive intervention and my part in Elizabeth having a less than successful practicum.

A Pilot Project: A Different Story

Novice teachers are amazing—dedicated, persistent, focused, idealistic, caring, creative, often tired, sometimes perplexed; they are on a roller coaster ride of highs and lows with their students and lesson plans. (Read about Susan in Marlowe and Page, 2005.) But they are awesome. Really *awesome!* And, as director of a very large and complex research project (Page, 1999; Page et al., 2001) involving 16 schools in three school districts in the state of Washington, it was a great opportunity and a tremendous honor for me to be able to work with over 200 first-, second-, and third-year teachers.

The Purpose of the Project

This pilot project was one of several in the state, the purpose of which was to align teacher performance standards with the student learning standards—in that state known as EALRs or Essential Academic Learning Requirements—and to develop the performance requirements for the new state Professional Certification requirements. (Teachers in Washington are now required to earn Professional Certification within their first five years of teaching and initial certification [Office of the Superintendent of Public Instruction, 2007].)

Three Phases

This particular pilot consisted of three phases. For the 16 schools, Phase 1 provided on-site mentor support as well as several issue-focused workshops for first-year teachers and their mentors (over 400 teachers altogether). Phase 2, which applied to the biggest district in the project, extended an earlier Apple School of Tomorrow program and allowed second-year teachers to contact advisors on a regular basis and also to take a week-long retreat from their classes to work through a particular problem, on-site, with those advisors. During the summer of Phase 3, each teacher in a select cohort chosen from the three school districts had to develop a Professional Growth Plan (PGP) that would address weaknesses and define new challenges in relation to the multiple criteria of the three proposed new state teacher performance standards: effective teaching, professional growth, and leadership (recently changed to professional contribution). The PGP was a combination of graduate course work and inservice programs that would extend to the end of the following summer.

BEN

The Context

When I first met Ben, he had just become one of the cohort of 17 teachers from the three school districts to participate in

Phase 3 of the project. It was the end of his second year of teaching world history in a ninth-grade class in a blue-collar, industrial area. It was obvious from his interviews with the project's researcher, and simply from talking to him, that he loved teaching and he loved his students who were 80 percent White and a combined 20 percent of Latino, Asian, Black, and American Indian.

Also from our conversations, from his initial project interviews, and from interviews with his Phase 1 and Phase 2 mentors, it was clear that Ben had worked hard to manage his classes and had made a lot of progress. By all accounts, from the beginning, he had had a command of names and knew how to use them; he also was skilled at asking directed questions. His language was never a problem; his speech was and had been professional and clear. His pace was excellent and his rapport with the students was strong. As a result of his hard work, awareness, and diligence, there wasn't mayhem in his classes; students were generally well behaved and attentive, and they didn't go out of their way to be disruptive or to distract others.

Ben's Issue

In his Professional Growth Plan, Ben chose four areas of focus, one of which—surprisingly—was classroom management. What Ben was struggling the most with was getting students to work in groups and to stay on task without interrupting other students or constantly asking him to repeat or to re-explain what they should be doing. His typical routine was to give the class the goals and instructions of the group work, then ask if there were any questions, respond to the students who had questions, and then set everyone loose to do the work. The results were always the same. Barely a minute would pass and a student would raise his or her hand and ask, "What exactly did you mean by . . . ?"

Ben would re-explain the instructions or try to clarify the task. In another couple of minutes, another student would jump up and hover over Ben's desk and plead, "I don't understand what you want us to do in this part. Should I . . . ?" Again, Ben would re-explain. Then there would be disagreements within groups as to what exactly they were supposed to be doing. More interruptions. Voices would get louder, with one student in a group trying to talk over another.

What this boiled down to each time was a disrupted and disjointed learning experience at best. At worst, there was little student learning and much side-talking, confusion, annoyance, and arguing. For Ben, it was disappointment that he worked so hard on creative lessons to have them fall so flat, for students to be so distressed and to learn so little. How could Ben fix this problem?

WHAT ARE WE SUPPOSED TO DO?

It's something you need to do many times a day: give clear directions and instructions. Not all teachers are equal; not all give intelligible directions; some trip over their own words (see Chapter 3) or ask questions that provide no way of knowing if students understand the task or not (Chapter 2); and some simply don't check for student understanding and then set the students to work.

In a flurry of confusion and misunderstandings, and as was happening in Ben's class, some students get frustrated and interrupt other on-task students by asking the teacher questions to clarify the task. "Did you mean . . . ?" "What if I . . . ? "What are we supposed to do?" Other students don't bother to ask the teacher; they just poke a friend and ask that person, again disrupting other students in the class; others just try to work, get frustrated and anxious, and eventually act out in any number of disruptive ways. Depending on certain activities, such as the game format in Elizabeth's class, some students simply go wild. This is not the environment in which students work or learn well. You don't want to be giving unclear directions that lead to confusion or worse. You want to give clear, comprehensible directions and you want to check for student understanding of those directions.

GIVING INSTRUCTIONS
THAT DON'T LEAD TO DISRUPTION

There are five steps to eliminating the confusion and disruption that can ensue once students begin a task.

1. Give the directions verbally.

2. Display these directions in some way—through a projector and PowerPoint slide, on newsprint hung on the wall, written on the board, or printed on a sheet handed out to students.

3. *The most critical step.* After you have explained the directions verbally, ask two students to re-explain the instructions in their own words. It is very important that the students do not repeat verbatim what you have said. That will not indicate understanding; it will just indicate repeating.

WHY IT'S IMPORTANT FOR
STUDENTS TO RE-EXPLAIN

Without this third step, you will most likely still have disruption in your classroom once the students begin their work. You will think you have explained well, and perhaps you have. And you will think the students can review the printed, displayed, or projected instructions. And maybe they will. But, neither your verbal directions nor your displayed visual directions are sufficient to prevent disruption and disorder in the classroom. What you need to know is whether or not students *understand* your directions and whether or not they understand what they ought to be doing and how they ought to be doing it.

Forget About Asking:
"Does Everyone Understand?"

Asking "Does everyone understand?" will cause only more confusion. Why? What kind of a question is "Does everyone understand?" (Hint: Check Chapter 2.) . . . It is an *anonymous question*. And it is the worst kind of anonymous question. It is a worthless question in terms of you, the teacher, getting the information you need to have—it doesn't give you information about student understanding of the directions. You will hear some students mumbling and you won't understand what they are saying. You will also hear some students saying "yes." That will be deceiving in that you have no idea if they really do or do not understand. You don't even necessarily know who they are.

You will also see different body language including heads down, heads shaking "yes," heads shaking "no," wiggling bodies, and all kinds of facial distortions and grimaces. You won't know what those signals mean. You don't have the information you need. You don't know who understands and who doesn't. If you set the students to work at this point, *you* will have caused and *you* will be to blame for the confusion and disruption that will follow.

Forget About Asking:
"Are There Any Questions?"

What kind of question is "Are there any questions?" (Hint: Again, check Chapter 2.) It is a *dangling question*. The students don't know what they are supposed to do with this question. Should they yell out? And if several yell out, how will you know who is yelling out what and who hasn't yelled out anything at all? And, if some shout out or shake their heads "no," what information does that give you? Almost none. It doesn't tell you who understands and who doesn't and, most importantly, it also doesn't tell you where or what the misunderstandings might be.

The students are frustrated with this question always because they have no clear or defined way to let you know their particular understanding or misunderstanding. There are also many students who simply will not respond to this kind of question, either because they are shy, don't want to look foolish or incompetent, or because they realize that a "yes" or "no" is not going to clarify the issues. Maybe you are assuming with your question, that if students have a question, they will raise their hands and ask you. A big mistake, if you want to prevent classroom disorder and disruption, is to make assumptions. Assumptions are often false. In Ben's classes, some students would raise their hands when he asked, "Are there any questions?" But even though Ben responded to those questions, all the unasked questions and hidden confusions remained and became the gremlins once the task began.

BACK UP! WE ARE MISSING TWO PRELIMINARY STEPS

First: An Explanation

Before you start to give *task* directions, explain how the process of giving the directions will work. Clarify that you are going to ask two students to explain the task in their own words after you finish giving the instructions. This practice will accomplish three very important things:

1. Students will realize they have to pay attention because you may be calling on them for re-explanation.

2. You will be having individual interaction with at least two students and will be able to very quickly determine if there are misunderstandings in the task instructions.

3. The rest of the class can rehear the directions in other words.

Once you have explained how this process will work (as above), by name, call on the first student to explain the procedure in his or her own words. If you think the explanation is solid and that the student understands, then go to the second student by name and ask him or her to clarify or add to this explanation or provide the explanation of how this will work.

If you think there is still confusion over how the process of giving the task directions will work, then you need to start all over. And then, again, ask two students for their own explanations. You need to do this until you are sure that the students understand the process. It's important to remember to explain why you will be doing this.

Second: Students Need to Ask Questions Up Front

To ensure that students will be on task, will be clear in the task, and will not disrupt or interrupt you or other students during the task, there is one more thing to do before you give the task instructions. Once the students understand that you will be asking them to re-explain the directions in their own words, you also will tell them that once they begin the task, they will not be asking you or any other students questions about the task, and that you will not answer their questions if they do ask them. This may sound mean, but it is the opposite.

Detrimental and Misplaced Caring

A teacher's job is to help students learn and to make students independent learners. A teacher's job is not to make students dependent. Student and novice teachers, especially, tend to be overly eager to assist students and, unintentionally, they don't let students learn for themselves. Instead, the teachers jump very quickly to give the students the answers or to regive directions over and over after the initial instructions. This is detrimental caring. Aside from exhausting the teacher, it leads to students becoming very lazy and very unsure students who are dependent on the teacher and cannot complete or understand tasks, or solve problems, without a teacher's close assistance (Gardner, 1991). Students will lose the ability to think for themselves about the problem or task— they will be looking for the teacher's answer.

In your explanation for this change in the classroom, it is important that you clarify your confidence in the students' abilities and the need for them to continue to develop their abilities to work without asking questions—they need to figure out things. They don't need to rely on you.

Up Front

If students are accustomed to your instant answers, constant and easy-to-get attention, and assistance, it will take some dedicated time and re-explanation as to why they should not expect answers to questions once they begin the task. Clarify that all their questions about the task and directions need to be up front before they set to work. Two things will result:

> **Students Learn to Not Think**
>
> *Sad, but true. By the time most students finish first grade, schooling and the emphasis on right answers has taught them to not think. (Gardner, 1991)*

1. As long as the students understand this policy and the reasons for it, they will pay more attention when you do give the directions.

2. They will ask questions willingly before the task begins.

But the ultimate result is that you will have a classroom of students who learn how to concentrate, realize they can do the work, feel more self-assured, rely less and less on your input and answers, stay on task, refrain from disruption and interruption of others, and, yes, learn.

BEN'S PLAN

Ben spent part of the Phase 3 summer program analyzing how his approach to giving directions was not working and how he could put a new plan into action during the fall term.

The Barbarian Hordes

Ben jumped into designing his plan with passion and enthusiasm. He knew immediately which topic he would choose for the experiment. Ben loved world history, particularly the era of the Roman Empire, and he loved the excitement about the topic that he could generate among the students. During his first two years of teaching he had developed several lesson plans on the topic that involved the students working in groups. One of his favorite plans focused on the barbarian invasions of the Roman Empire. That was the plan he would repeat, except this time he would implement the five steps for giving directions.

Following the Steps

Ben began the lesson by writing the instructions on the whiteboard before the class came into the room. The instructions read:

---

1. Each group will represent one of the barbarian hordes which invaded the Roman Empire.

2. The group will develop the arguments and reasons why they believe they alone were responsible for the fall of the Roman Empire.

3. The group will explain the arguments to the class.

The first thing Ben did was to explain that before the students could begin the task, he would be asking two of them to restate the directions in their own words and that he would be doing this to ensure understanding and to avoid disruptions for all students. Just as important, he announced that all questions needed to be asked up front before the work began, and that once the group work began, no one could ask any questions of him. After several gasps from the students, he stated more than once how confident he was that they were able to do the work on their own. Then he asked two students (by name) to re-explain the process and they did.

Then he began. He explained verbally what was already written on the board and then. . . .

"Jen, Karen, Brian, and Sam, you will be the Huns."

"John, Sara, Breydon, and Taylor, you will be the Visigoths."

"Nate, Matt, Ocean, and Amy, you will be the Vandals."

"Greg, Tony, Nicollette, and Aria, you will be the Franks."

"Violet, Tom, Joaquim, Bill, and the other Matt, you will be the Burgundians."

"Daren, Leah, Tina, and Sasha, you will be the Ostragoths."

This time Ben did not ask, as he would have previously, "Are there any questions?" Instead, he called on Nicollette to re-explain the instructions and the task. Nicollette gave a clear description of the project. Then Ben asked Matt if he understood the directions. When he answered, "Yes," Ben responded with, "Great, please re-explain it to all of us." And Matt did.

That done, Ben then reminded them that he wouldn't answer any questions once they began their work, but that he would answer any questions before they began. He waited . . . hands went up everywhere. Ben responded to all of the questions until he once again reminded the students, there wouldn't be any interruptions once they began their work. There were no more questions. Ben finished by posing the most important question of all: "Why do this learning experience on the Barbarian hordes at all?" After several in-depth and critical responses from the students, Ben set them free.

The Time Factor

Yes, this had taken about five minutes' worth of time and it may take more in different classes. This is hardly the amount of time that would have been wasted had the students disrupted each other and the group work with their questions.

The students began their work, and, according to Ben, they were the most focused he had seen them in group work. There were two students who forgot; they raised their hands and Ben

Choices

Your choices are to spend several minutes making sure the students understand task directions or to jump right into the task and waste most of the working time with frustrations and distractions.

Misinterpretations

If you have a class of 30 students, and you give instructions for a task, how many of those students will interpret the directions in the way that you mean them? According to Piaget (Labinowicz, 1980; Piaget, 1941/1995), probably one student, if you are lucky. This is because you and the students do not have mutual communication frameworks. Students hear what they perceive and what connects to their past experiences and that might not be the same thing as what you say or mean—yet another reason to take the time to clarify instructions and to make students responsible for understanding the instructions and for asking questions before the task begins.

reminded them, "Sorry, I can't answer any questions. I know you will figure it out." They went right back to work with an "oh, we forget" look on their faces.

THE RESULTS

The result was not just focused, on-task work with no distractions or disruptions, but when the students came to the front of the room with their arguments, in Ben's view, they were more confident than usual and their responses were much more in-depth and analytical than usual and than he had expected. My observation was that it was an outstanding lesson.

SPECIAL NEEDS

Besides the probability that only 1 student out of 30 may understand your initial instructions, there is another important issue to consider. Students with special needs often have learning disabilities that typically manifest as comprehension deficits. These comprehension problems exacerbate the difficulties associated with understanding and following directions. You may be shocked at the difference that the processes of students re-explaining instructions and asking questions up front make in the attitude, task orientation, and success of these (as well as all other) students. They will be able to work without their usual angst about what it is they are supposed to be doing and without feeling that they are the only ones who don't understand. They will no longer have to feel singled out for clarification of the task, no longer will have to feel foolish if they have a question, will be able to begin the work with the rest of the class, will stay more focused, will gain in self-confidence, and ultimately will disrupt the class less, if at all, and learn more. Everyone wins in this new learning environment.

Depending on your class format, students with more severe and complex needs may require special accommodations. For discussion on the most productive class formats for students with special needs, please see Chapter 9 in Marlowe and Page, 2005.

SUMMARY: STEP 4

1. Explain the procedure; that is, you will give directions, students will re-explain in their own words, then students may ask questions before beginning the work. Once the task begins you won't answer any questions.

2. Have two students explain this process in their own words.

3. Give the task instructions.

4. Display the task instructions visually in clear view for all students or hand out copies.

5. By name, call on one student to re-explain task directions in his or her own words.

6. By name, call on a second student to re-explain directions or to clarify or expand on what the first student says.

7. If student understanding is not sufficient, start the process over.

8. When you are confident the students understand the task, re-explain that they may not ask questions once the task begins because it is disruptive to others and because they have the ability to do this without asking the questions.

9. Ask students to raise hands if there are still questions before the task begins.

10. Once there are no more questions, set the students to the task and then remind them again that you won't answer questions—they will have to figure it out themselves.

11. Students with severe needs may need special accommodations.

You may be thinking, why not condense this list of steps for giving directions. Sorry, there are no shortcuts here.

WHAT'S NEXT?

Chapter 5 explains, in general, why different classes require different amounts of attention to behavior issues and, in particular, how to avoid the problems that can occur every time there is a transition or new task in the classroom.

5

Attending to Civility With Reminders and Cues

SEVENTH PERIOD: A SPECIAL NINTH-GRADE CLASS

It was January. The teacher whose place I was taking had suddenly and inexplicably left. I looked over the rosters for my new classes in my new job in this small (450 students), almost completely White (96 percent) suburban high school in a town of approximately 14,000 and I saw four classes with over 30 students each and one ninth-grade class with only 17 students. This school did not rotate the class periods, so I knew I would have this small class the last period each day; the class would be 45 minutes. "What did I do to deserve such a perfect end to each day?" I asked myself.

THE FIRST DAY OF SCHOOL

Other than being very large, the four classes leading up to the last period of the day were fairly ordinary and nothing stuck out as being problematic. Then it was time for the smaller class. As was required, I stood at the doorway on guard duty as the students began to enter the room.

Whoa!

All hell broke loose. Aaron, the first student who entered, looking more like a senior than a freshman in both size and general appearance, ran into the room, jumped onto a chair, then to another, and another, and another, all while flicking his "Bic" lighter so that the flame was about eight inches high. This jumping was not easy. The chairs were attached to desks. The rest of the students ran into the room in a helter skelter fashion pushing and shoving, knocking over desks, and creating a noise that sounded like a tornado approaching. Or was it a runaway train? In any case, that was how the class began. The rest of the class period went downhill from there.

Fourteen IEPs

It didn't take long to discover that of the 17 students, 14 were students with special needs, each one with an Individual Education Plan (IEP). It was strange how this information was not revealed at the time of my interview. In any case, there was no aide in the room, nor would there be one. This class turned out to be the biggest challenge I had faced in several years of teaching.

WHAT HAPPENED WITH THIS CLASS?

It would take another book to describe everything that happened in this class. (On a side note, I did learn that the previous teacher had had a nervous breakdown and that is why there was an opening in January.) It was very slow going, with very small progress one day, only to take several steps back the next. Halfway through the semester, Aaron, who had gotten two young women at the school pregnant, was arrested for stealing cars. All but three students who were quiet and looked scared most of the time continued to act out in a variety of ways including one student throwing a chair through the window. One day when I was at my wit's end, I had a conversation with another teacher about this class. Her advice became very important to my managing the issues and behaviors in the class.

It's not that I didn't know this already; it's not that you don't know it already. But teachers need reminders sometimes also. It is Mrs. Watkins's advice that is the grounding for this chapter, which focuses on teaching about, reminding students about, and providing cues for civility.

MRS. WATKINS'S ADVICE

Classes Have Different Needs

Mrs. Watkins reminded me that no two classes are alike and that some students come to school with much more baggage than others. This baggage can range from poverty, to mental or physical illness, to disadvantaged or abusive home lives, to cultural, learning, and language differences. Depending on how the issues differ and play out in a class, and therefore lead to different classroom management concerns, you have to spend different amounts of class time, she advised, on teaching simple expectations and behaviors of civility. For the classes who have few behavior issues, you will be able to focus on academic content for about 90 percent of the time. For the other 10 percent of the time, you may have to attend to behavior concerns. For the classes that have distorted and skewed dynamics, as my seventh period class did, it could be the reverse: You might need to spend 90 percent of your time teaching or reminding students how to behave civilly and therefore will be able to spend only 10 percent of your time on academic content.

Horrified?

Of course you want all students to have an equal opportunity to learn. To suggest otherwise is ludicrous. The problem is that if you do not provide and maintain a safe and civil environment in your classroom, little learning of any significant value will occur anyway. Your efforts and time spent teaching academics in a disordered or chaotic class will not only be pretty much wasted but are also a signal that you lack awareness of the classroom dynamics or don't know what to do about it. You can't teach, and students can't learn, over disruption, distractions, and chaos. Some classes simply need more attention before academics are even possible (Brophy, 1996). Anyone who has worked in distressed schools or with disturbed classes understands the need to spend much time and effort on civility. Success in teaching is not always (and should never solely be) measured by students' academic rankings.

In this seventh period class, Mrs. Watkins's reminders rang too true and I did have to spend a lot of the time working on issues of civil behavior, over and over again. Was there academic learning? Yes, a little. Was the class safe? Yes. Nervous breakdown? Close, but no.

THE PROBLEM WITH CLASSROOM RULES

By the time you are reading this book, you probably already have heard and read a lot about the different ways of setting up classroom rules and procedures. At the elementary level, whether developed by teacher or teacher and students together, the "rules" usually sound something like this:

1. Be respectful.

2. Listen when the teacher talks.

3. Follow school rules.

4. Walk in the halls and classroom.

5. Raise your hands to talk.

6. Be courteous.

At the secondary level, rules might look like the following:

1. Get to class on time.

2. Bring required materials to class.

3. Use appropriate language.

4. Be respectful.

While some research results emphasize the need for clear teaching of classroom rules at the beginning of the school year (Morine-Dershimer, 2006), other research shows that adolescents, especially, can resent and think of authoritarian rules as arbitrary (Turiel, 1983) and rebel against them.

Can You Define Respect?

The problem with these rules is that they don't work. In 20 years of observing in hundreds of classrooms, I have yet to see these *rules* have much effect on or in any classroom. Most of them are too vague to have any meaning to students. "Be respectful" is often lost on elementary students altogether, even after much discussion as to what it means. In several elementary schools, I have asked students to define "respectful." The answers have ranged from "not swearing," to "not hitting," to "being kind." In one school, when I asked a first grader, "What does *kind* mean?" the answer was "not hitting." With the majority of students, there was no real sense of the word "respect"; students, instead, would latch onto single pieces of behavior that might be an element of respect. It's too global a word—too global a concept for students to think about, understand, and practice for six hours of the day. "Follow school rules," similarly, is too vague. What are the school rules, anyway? What does the word "respect" mean to you?

Lack of Consistency

At the middle and high school level, there is the problem not only of the vagueness—what *is* appropriate language in this class? and what exactly *are* the required materials every day?—but also the problem that every class has its own rules and every time a student leaves class A, he has to attend five or six other classes (maybe fewer if there is block scheduling), all with their own rules, and go through about 24 hours before he arrives once again in class A. If the school has block scheduling, it may be three days before he is back in class A again. (See Chapter 1 for other differences between elementary, middle, and secondary school days.)

High school students, in particular, have way too much going on in their lives to pay much attention to all these sets of rules on any sustained basis. Additionally, adolescents begin to look for more autonomy and control as their cognitive capabilities advance (Bandura, 1986). What is clear is that in order to learn, all students need teachers who are able to maintain order, provide limits for behavior, and create an environment in which all students feel safe (Cothran et al., 2003). Students want teachers to provide clarity, structure, and limits in the classroom and they have little appreciation for teachers who are too permissive (Weinstein & Mignano, 2003).

SIMPLE EXPECTATIONS OF CIVILITY

Given the ineffectiveness of lists of rules in gaining and sustaining a classroom environment free of disorder and one conducive to learning, this chapter focuses on a more productive approach. This chapter is an extension of, or overlap to, Chapter 3, which discusses the need for constantly teaching and using words of civility. And, it is about how necessary it is to remind students, to give them cues, continually, about how to act in a civil way in your classroom. K–12 students are not the only ones who act disrespectfully, thoughtlessly, or inappropriately in a classroom. Teachers in graduate classes often display the same kinds of behaviors. When students of any age are together in a confined space for a·substantial time period, they can act in ways that range from down right ridiculous to outrageously obnoxious to extremely dangerous.

JEANNIE

Jeannie knew from the time she was in high school that she wanted to teach in an inner city high school, so when she learned that her student teaching placement was in a large inner city high school in a metropolitan area of approximately four million people, she was energized and excited.

The Context

Just getting into and out of the school parking lot alive was an accomplishment. The only route in and out of the lot was through an area riddled with drive-by shootings. The parking lot had its own armed guard to protect the cars against vandalism, to ensure they wouldn't be stolen, to protect the teachers as they got into the building, and to keep unwanted visitors from loitering. There were chains and locks on all the doors and everyone had to ring a bell and go through security checks to enter. Once in the building, things seemed safer and calmer and even somewhat upbeat, but there were many undercurrents of racial tension in the school. It was obvious that the cleaning crew had tried to get graffiti off the lockers, but there were many remnants that were readable.

The classroom Jeannie had was a narrow and long room with a small window on the wall opposite the door. There were two long tables put together end to end and students sat around the extended table two rows deep. They were squashed into the room; they had no space for anything; and only the students in the first row had use of the table top. It was hot, and the air quality was poor.

The Class

Jeannie was teaching American literature in the tenth grade. There were 39 students in her class—evenly divided among Black, Latino, and Asian students. Unfortunately there was tension in Jeannie's class. As she explained it, and as I observed it and captured it on tape on my first visit, in general, the Asian students spoke very quietly when Jeannie called on them. They rarely volunteered. About half of the Latino and Black students were at loggerheads, it seemed, in some kind of an unannounced contest to outdo the other. They yelled at each other as they came into the room, and they made veiled and overt threats across the room at each other. They didn't wait for Jeannie to call on them. They yelled out questions, answers, or retaliatory comments. The Black and Latino students not involved in this daily melee made faces and noises of disgust as if they were embarrassed by these loud, aggressive, and threatening students.

The Issue

It didn't take long for Jeannie to grasp this problem. When a Latino student spoke or made a presentation, there were interruptions from some Black students; when a Black student presented, it was the opposite. These disruptions ranged from laughing, ridiculing, snickering, and swearing, to making distracting noises to rattle the student. When an Asian student responded or presented, the room remained quiet.

The main issue was the contention among the two rival groups of students. During my first visit, Jeannie was visibly shaken trying to quiet these interruptions and she made it clear in our discussion after class that she realized the class was not going to work in any meaningful way if she couldn't figure out how to quell the outbursts. She also knew she needed to create an environment in which all of the students could, and would want to, work together. Her goals were to help the Asian students feel safer and be more involved and to require civil behavior of the offending students.

Jeannie knew little about the backgrounds of the students. She did know, from the mentor teacher, that two of the male students were living out of their cars and that several students knew only one parent. She knew from what she overheard herself in class that some of the male students talked often about guns and shootings. She also knew that she couldn't control what happened outside of the school, but that she had to make changes within her own classroom. What would you do if you were Jeannie? How would you change this classroom dynamic? Were school rules impacting behavior in this class? Think about the following.

REMINDERS AND CUES

Students are not mind readers. Students need calm, constant, and consistent reminding of, or cues to, what is appropriate in a classroom setting. In order to prevent disruption and disorder in the classroom, in addition to implementing the previous Steps 1 through 4, a teacher or student has to clearly state civil and simple behavior requirements at the beginning of each new task and for each transition in class. These verbal cues can be very short and quick, but they need to be crystal clear and, frequently, as with giving instructions and directions, re-explained by one or two students in their own words to confirm understanding. Here are some examples:

1. "Now you are going to get into groups to complete the project you began yesterday. Please *move silently* and *begin the work immediately without chatting.* Thank you."

This is clear, very quick, concise, reminds the students what they need to do, and is now fresh in their minds. If you omit these cues, you can't expect that the students will move silently or that they will begin the work immediately without chatting. They are human. Most likely they will not be silent and will in fact begin chatting immediately; you will blame the students for the indiscretions, when, in reality, they are just acting their age, enjoying the opportunity to move around, and it is your omission of requirements that has led to the unwanted behavior.

2. "We are going to start our work on science now. Please *return to your seats silently* [if that is what you expect] and *without banging into the desks.* Thank you. I appreciate it."

Middle school students love to bump into each other and the furniture. The specific language you use will depend on the age and grade of the student and on what problems have already played out in the class.

    3. "Susan, please remind the class what has to happen as we get ready for lunch. Thank you."

If Susan is unable to explain the procedures and the specific expected behaviors, ask another student to help her.

    4. "We will begin as soon as everyone is *silent and focused*. Thank you."

Revisit Chapter 3 for the explanation of the difference between the word "silent" and the word "quiet" and resulting student behavior. Rarely do students think *quiet* means *silent*. If silence is what you want, you will have to use the word "silence" or "silent" depending on the context.

How Often Do You Have to Give Reminders or Cues?

Buckle your safety belt. Unless your class has no pulse and never behaves in unwanted ways, if you want to prevent disorder, confusion, lack of concentration, disruption, or just lively students raising a rumpus in your classroom, you will need to give quick and friendly reminders or cues every time there is a transition or new task. Novice teachers and preservice teachers who are in their first practicum tend to feel and look rather awkward doing this. But pre and post videotapes of such actions show the difference in classroom flow, dynamic, and on-task behavior when teachers use these simple directives. Those who omit the civil expectations or procedure explanations pay every time when they have to interrupt the class to remind students about what they should be doing or how they should be behaving. Did these ideas impact Jeannie and her class?

JEANNIE'S APPROACH

What Jeannie did to rectify her situation was to explain to the students what she saw as problematic in the classroom, tell them why the class couldn't continue in that way, and state that she was going to make some changes, which would include reminding students before each presentation that there wouldn't be any distractions, talking, or ridiculing. The other change was that everyone in the class would be required to abandon their derogatory words and instead use words of civility. She prepared for my second visit.

The Lesson

Jeannie had developed a creative plan for analyzing the book, *Catcher in the Rye* (Salinger, 1951). Students had finished reading the book (mostly in class since some of the students would not complete homework assignments) and were to select a part of the book that had meaning to them. They would then put that excerpt on a transparency and when it was their turn, go to the overhead projector, display the selection, and explain to the class why they had chosen that particular excerpt and what meaning it had to them.

Jeannie's Reminders and Cues

Before Jeannie called on Carlos to go to the overhead, she gave the necessary cues.

"Everyone will remain *silent* and *attentive* to Carlos while he is presenting. Thank you."

Carlos came to the projector and began to talk. Students were focused and behaving for most of Carlos' presentation, but toward the end, there was some undistinguishable noise from one of the students in the opposing group. Jeannie quietly, smoothly, and quickly said, "Jackson . . . please . . . Thank you." That was all she had to say and Carlos continued almost uninterrupted.

Once again Jeannie directed, "Everyone will be *silent* and *attentive* to Rana as she presents. Thank you."

This time things were quiet throughout the presentation. Liah was next and again Jeannie reminded the students. Again there were no interruptions. Next was Chavonne and again Jeannie inserted the reminders. This time there was another interruption and again, Jeannie simply said, "Ramone . . . please." and then, "Thank you."

Not only, then, did Jeannie learn that she would have to explain and remind students of appropriate civil behavior at every task change, but that she would have to also do it every time there was a transition as a new student presented or responded. When students have little or no experience with words of civility or general norms of classroom or civil behavior, it takes constant and much effort to help them change their behavior.

THE RESULTS

It took the whole practicum for Jeannie to create an environment of safety for everyone. The disruptions and threats lessened, but things were not perfect. The Asian students became more active, although not as much as Jeannie would have liked. The issue of behavior among the opposing students was more difficult. There was still an underlying tension that felt to Jeannie as if it would explode at any moment. It didn't. Jeannie had at least made inroads to students working together and to civility. She felt safer; the students felt safer. The class was ready for learning.

THE BOTTOM LINE

The bottom line is that while giving constant behavior reminders and cues may seem tedious, ridiculous, or just plain unnecessary, you will discover it saves you a great deal of time, headache, class disruption, and mayhem in the class. It doesn't take long for giving quick verbal reminders or cues to become second nature for you; in action it takes only seconds to carry out. The major benefit is that students learn to use words of civility and learn about civil behavior. In the long run, they have more time and proclivity for academic learning.

Experienced teachers are shocked when they try this and find how easy it is to make the change and how dramatic the change in their classroom is. Evidence suggests that more than 30 separate activities occur each day in the average elementary school class (Ross, 1984). At the middle and high schools, with several different instructional periods and with multiple teachers, students leave and enter classrooms several times a day and have different transitions, tasks, and expectations within each class. Students can't remember it all. Students need the reminders; they need the cues.

SUMMARY: STEP 5

1. Provide concise and quick verbal reminders of expected civil behavior before every task and transition.

2. Choose your words carefully. If you want silence, you have to use that word.

3. Ask students to re-explain expectations of civility.

COMING NEXT

Chapter 6 provides critical ways to develop and increase fluid classroom relationships, connections, and communication— all of which are essential to creating a sense of safety, belonging, class community, and a student's desire to be in your class rather than out of it. Having a class that is interactive goes a long way to eliminating and preventing disorder and disruption in the classroom and, most importantly, to creating the culture that allows and promotes high student engagement. It is not for the faint of heart.

6

Upgrading Interactions

Can You Feel the Heartbeat?

THE TITLE

As explained in the Introduction, the title, *You Can't Teach Until Everyone Is Listening,* refers to the need for the teacher to pay attention to what is happening in the class, to be able to *hear* whether or not the class dynamic enhances each student's well being and is beneficial or not to learning. Without hearing and attending to this, the teacher can't expect to have students who feel safe, who feel that they belong, and who are themselves then able to listen, be attentive, and be engaged, and who do not negatively impact the class.

Chapters 1 through 5 have defined five proactive steps that are essential to establishing this safe and positive classroom— one with minimal disruptions, distractions, and misbehavior. However, while safe and positive is great, it is not enough if you want to have an incredibly dynamic class, one defined by exceptional student engagement, interaction, and learning. And who doesn't want an incredibly dynamic class? Julia wanted it.

Julia

Julia was a student teacher at an affluent high school in a small, suburban city of approximately 20,000. The makeup of the student population was approximately 87 percent White, 7 percent Asian, and 6 percent Latino and Black (most of whom were bussed in daily from the inner city). The town was and is known as a bedroom community for professionals.

The Context

Julia was teaching United States history to eleventh graders. The whole school was in distress because not only had both the principal and vice principal been having affairs with the principal's secretary, but the local and big city newspapers were having a field day with the story and had spread it all over the front pages; there was pandemonium in the school. At any time, anything can happen to alter the culture and ethos of the school, but this is irrelevant, because it is still the teacher's job to conduct the class, to prevent disruption and disorder, to keep students safe, and to develop and provide experiences through which the students will learn.

Julia was doing a good job as a student teacher. She had already mastered the skill of using students' names; she avoided anonymous and dangling questions; her language was professional, tight, and fast-paced; she made sure that students understood directions; and she was clear to her students about how transitions would occur. Still, there was a restlessness in the class, as Julia described it, that was coming in every day from the hallways and was disturbing the flow and attention of the class. Students were gossiping continually and taking advantage of the disarray in the principals' offices. To Julia, her students seemed very distracted and agitated. What did Julia need to do to get the class back on track, keep it focused, and propel it forward?

Videotaping Julia's Class

We videotaped Julia's class and reviewed the tape together. What was apparent was that Julia needed to increase the amount of interaction she was having with all of her students. The agitation in her class was not just a result of the extended hallway gossip. Julia, herself, was playing a role in this unrest as her interactions with students were not even. She wasn't drawing all the students into the class conversations and discussions equally (or with a purpose of in-depth thinking) and those not involved or less involved were still stuck in that schoolwide issue. Part of her class was breathing and with her, while the other part was needing a shot of adrenalin and redirection.

MOVING TO A HIGHER LEVEL

It was time for Julia, and now it is time for you, to take a huge leap forward in managing your classroom. Upgrading interactions is probably the most difficult of the Six Steps and focuses on intensifying and multiplying positive and productive teacher–to–student and student–to–student interactions. It will require diligence, consistent effort, awareness, persistence, and the desire to do it. In addition, depending on where you are with managing your class(es), it may require that you get considerably outside of your comfort zone. With the solid foundation of Steps 1 through 5 on which to build, however, upgrading interactions will help you create a high impact learning environment, the by-product of which will be reduction or elimination of lingering classroom disorder.

The Heart and Soul and a Rhythm and a Beat

It's simple. The heart and soul of teaching and learning are the relationships and interactions between and among you and the students (Bandura, 1996; McCaslin & Good, 1996; Schneider, 1992; Shin, Daly, & Vera, 2007; Wentzel & Watkins, 2002), but productive and positive relationships and interactions don't just happen. Think of yourself as an orchestra conductor and picture yourself conducting a large group of students as they interact to play a symphony together. As the book title suggests, you have to listen to the sounds of your class. Once you have developed vibrant interactions in your class, you will be able to hear the amazing music; you will be able to hear a rhythm and a beat, a momentum and a heartbeat, if you will, that are enormously inviting and electric. The rhythm and the beat of Julia's class were neither. They were jagged at best and needed fixing.

CHALLENGING JULIA

Two Challenges

I challenged Julia first to interact verbally with every student at least three times in a classroom period for the next week. (There were approximately 30 students in each of her classes and the class periods were 45 minutes long.) Julia confided to me later, after she had completed her practicum and received her grade, that she had thought I was crazy.

As if that weren't enough, the secondary challenge for Julia was to develop student-to-student interaction to improve the sense of whole communication in the class, to improve each student's sense of belonging, and ultimately to raise the level of thinking in such a way that her class would sound like it was humming. She was to do that by asking one student to respond to another whenever possible. After a week of working on the challenges, we videotaped Julia's class again and this tape showed that the classroom was a very different place.

Increased Interaction

Julia's first attempts at more individual interaction were awkward and seemed forced. But by the end of the week, Julia was doing it effortlessly. She was fast. "Susie, what are your conclusions . . . " and "Todd, How can you add to that?" and "Adam, Why would that be a problem?" She worked on her verbal and eye contact with the students for the first two days and then went to the next step of developing and increasing student-to-student interaction.

"Gerry, please explain to Susie how you would add to what she said. Please make eye contact with Susie as you speak. Thank you." And "Tim, please respond to what John said and look at John while you are doing that." And then, raising the thinking stakes, "Brittany, ask Connor a critical question that will lead him to think about that issue in other ways" (Marlowe & Page, 2005). You could start to feel the heartbeat.

THE RESULTS

The pace had picked up considerably and student attention was high, focused, and positive. The class energy, as a whole, had multiplied dramatically. This experiment was not without incident. The students found it very difficult to make eye contact with one another and tended to break down giggling. That needed more work. But students, of their own initiative, were contributing to a much greater degree than previously. Even more importantly, students were discussing issues in depth with each other. The heartbeat was getting healthier and gaining in strength.

For the time being, the student-to-student interaction was at Julia's direction and discretion, but that too would change as the semester progressed. By my last visit to Julia's class, it was a completely different place. Julia's energy had tripled. She looked like a successful, experienced teacher; best of all, the students were more "with it," more connected, and clearly more together as a class. They were making suggestions on a regular basis on how they could work together on research, in discussions, and even in writing articles for the school newspaper. They hardly needed Julia in the room. Her class had become a unique song. Now the heartbeat was obvious and powerful. Julia was a success and had multiple offers for jobs at the end of her practicum.

Two Challenges for You

1. Interact With Every Student Twice Every 50 or 60 Minutes

If you are an elementary teacher, the first challenge for you is to interact verbally with every student at least *twice* (I have mellowed) every hour. This will mean you have had approximately 12 direct (using name and eye contact) verbal contacts with each student each day. At the middle and high schools, for every 50-minute period or time slot, you will interact (name and make eye contact) with each student at least twice. Over the top? Try it.

2. Increase Student-to-Student Interaction

Your interaction with students is not enough. The second challenge is to develop and increase the interaction *among* students so that they will feel connected and that they belong—so that they will feel like they are capable, and so that they will be able to learn from each other in new ways.

For elementary teachers, try initially for 10 to 20 of these student-to-student interactions per day and build from there. For middle and secondary teachers, the initial goal should be to have as many student-to-student interactions as possible during one period (this will vary drastically depending on the students and the class and safety issues).

The ultimate goal is that sooner rather than later students have become so skilled at making these connections in a productive, civilized, and nondisruptive way, that highly engaged and high-level work occurs without your intervention. Once you have established and secured this foundation of connections and enhanced sense of belonging, you will be able to step aside more and more often without disorder and disruption reoccurring.

How to Begin

Videotape Your Class

As Julia did, videotape your class. But before you begin, you most likely will need permission. Explain to your principal that you are trying to increase positive interaction, student involvement, on-task behavior, and consequently, learning. Make sure that the principal knows the videotape is for instructional (your) purposes only and that it will not go anywhere else. Be prepared for different reactions:

1. Some principals give blanket permission to do this and there is no further permission needed. Many schools are used to having teachers videotape their classes especially if there is a student teacher in the class. Some states, including Kentucky, Connecticut, and New York (Connecticut State Department of Education, 2005; Jerald & Boser, 2000), even require it for all novice teachers.

2. The principal may agree as long as you get parental permission. This will mean that you need to send home a very short permission slip explaining that you will be taping the class for instructional purposes only. If there are parents who will not sign, then you have to make sure their children do not appear in the video.

3. The principal may say outright, "No." There may be a history of legal issues in your school, or in some schools there may be "protected" students, meaning that there are students who would be in danger if they were seen.

Assuming that you get permission, videotape your class as it now functions, then increase your interaction with the students and increase student-to-student interaction as the challenges above describe. Do that for a week and videotape your class again. Remember to explain to the students what you are doing and why; that is, you are increasing your interaction with them to make sure every one has an equal chance to be involved, to make sure you know who does and does not understand, to pick up the pace of the class, and to make the class a place they want to be and in which they can learn. Explain that you are increasing student-to-student interaction to create better connections among students and to have students learn more from each other. Compare the pre and post tapes, continue to work at increasing interaction, and then tape again.

You Can Learn a Lot From an Audiotape

If you are in a school where you cannot get permission to videotape your class, use an audiotape recorder. You will learn plenty from this. Place it in the back of the room and you will learn not only what you are doing and saying and whether you are increasing interaction or not but also how well the students can hear each other's responses. For example, if you have students in the front of the room responding to you, you may hear the response. But students sitting near the back of the room (near the audio recorder) may not hear much. If that is the case, you won't be able to hear much on the audiotape either and that means you have a problem that also can lead to disruption, disarray, confusion, and frustration in the classroom.

Students Who Can't Hear Are Potential Disrupters

If students in the back or other locations in the room cannot hear the student responses that are focused and directed at you or toward another student, then you need to make some changes. Students need to speak more clearly and loudly and you need to check frequently to determine if the students away from the speaking student can hear. You don't do this by asking, "Johnny, did you hear that?" That is the kind of question that gives you very little, if any, useful information. Johnny may say "yes," whether he has heard or not. Instead, ask him something about what was just said or ask him to say more about it to determine if, in fact, he has heard it. Students won't get involved, except in detrimental ways, if they can't hear.

WHAT CAN GO WRONG HERE?

There are all kinds of reasons teachers avoid individual interaction with students or do not encourage student-to-student
interaction. Some will say there just isn't time. Some will say
students need to be doing their own work. Some will say the
students are too immature to handle it. Some may say it is not
necessary. But the main reason, usually unspoken, is the dis-
comfort the teacher has in giving up some control. Teachers
can feel vulnerable when they can't predict how students will
react or respond to this kind of interaction.

Unwanted or Unexpected Responses

Novice and preservice teachers are the ones who avoid
interaction the most. By avoiding teacher-to-student interaction, particularly with marginal students, they believe they are
eliminating the chance that a student will give an incorrect,
inappropriate, or even confrontational response that will lead,
they think, to disruption or chaos or simply to them, the
teachers, not knowing how to react or what to say. By avoiding
student-to-student interaction, they are preventing, they are
sure, all kinds of cataclysmic behaviors including, at worst,
students getting out of control or, at best, students getting off
task. You do have to conquer these fears because lack of interaction, whatever your teaching experience level, leads to the
same problem that occurs when teachers focus on four or five
students in the classroom; that is, the class will have a lopsided
dynamic with all of the same issues Chapter 2 describes.

Dealing With Unexpected and
Unwanted Responses—See the Appendix

To help alleviate feelings of insecurity and trepidation at
the thought of increasing interaction, the Appendix to this
book provides four of the common, scary, or belligerent comments students may make as you begin this change. What the
students typically say is not unusual and it is not impossible
to handle. You just have to be aware of what they might say

and be ready with a quick, strong, and clear response. There-fore, the Appendix also presents responses that teachers have made to these student's comments. These are responses that have had positive results and that have allowed the teachers to continue upgrading and strengthening interactions without feeling threatened or vulnerable. It doesn't hurt to practice these responses in front of a mirror.

Students will stop trying to disrupt class with their delib-erate confrontational responses once they see that you are taking charge and that they can't divert you from your goal. It won't take very long for the class to get used to this new interactive process and you will be well on your way to hav-ing more consistent student attention, better and equal student participation, class community, fewer disruptions, and consequently real learning in your classroom.

Two Other Problems

There are, though, two other classroom situations to con-template that can impact your process and progress of up-grading interactions in your class and which define another kind of disorder in your classroom.

SUBTLE CLASSROOM DISORDER

Disorder and malcontent in the classroom do not come only in the obvious forms of raucousness, bigotry, disrespect, rude-ness, lack of attention, uneven or low student involvement as in Julia's class, or even, as discussed above, students trying to derail you from getting them involved. Classroom disorder also comes in more subtle, less overt forms that can be more difficult to identify and address, but which can be just as detri-mental to a student's or students' well being, to students' attention and learning, to your class's overall health, to your attempts at increasing classroom interaction, and to develop-ing a strong class momentum.

Consider shy or detached students (Brophy, 1996; Rosenberg, Wilson, Maheady, & Sindelar, 1992) who will do just about anything to stay on the fringes of the class and to avoid participating. Since your class is only as robust as its weakest link, you can't ignore these students and expect them to grow or expect to have an optimal and alive learning environment in which every student wants to and can be involved and interact. With students left on the sidelines of your class, you still have a classroom with, and in, disorder.

Please meet Jake.

JAKE

Jake was a ninth grader in my U.S. History class. I didn't realize initially how fearful he was of speaking in the class or even of being noticed by others in the class. Shrinking into oblivion was his goal. The first time he had to speak in front of the class, he ran from the room crying. No, it's not just third graders like Shalee who cry. So, after talking with Jake alone and then with the class, it was decided and agreed that Jake would start off making verbal presentations to the class, from behind the students, at the back of the room where he felt more comfortable.

As the year progressed, he moved one row closer to the front each time he had to speak to the class. Each time, he faced the front of the room, not the students. By the end of May, he had made it to the first row of the classroom, still facing the front of the room. As he prepared to speak, I asked him if he was ready and he replied, "Yes," and to everyone's surprise and to thunderous applause, he turned around and faced the students with a grin on his face. It was a huge triumph for him. It was an amazing event for the whole class. The class' heart was beating louder, much louder.

SHY STUDENTS

Shy students, most likely, will *not* welcome your increased interaction or attention and will not necessarily appreciate interaction with other students. Here is where you have to bring them into the classroom dynamic. You have the responsibility to engage with all students even if in different ways and even if they fight the involvement. All students need to feel confident or to gain confidence. Helping them find self-assurance by getting them to participate in the class in successful ways adds to their and the class' overall well being. In some cases, this may take the whole year to accomplish.

You will find your own ways to work with shy students, but just don't avoid them. It doesn't help them grow; it doesn't help them belong; it doesn't help them learn (Lacina-Gifford, 2001). And, it doesn't help to make your class a productive whole.

Detached Students

In addition to shy students, like Jake, there will be detached students (Geddes, 2007; Ottavi, 2007) who just don't want to or won't make connections with other students or with you. They won't want to cooperate at all. This next vignette is a story about two alienated and detached students. They had no friends in the class and didn't speak to anyone including each other. This self or otherwise imposed isolation and lack of connection to anyone was the subtle disorder in Phil's class and it came to light in a dramatic way when Phil involved his students in the National History Day program.

National History Day

National History Day (NHD) is a Grades 5 through 12 national program that focuses on students researching and analyzing a topic related to a yearly theme. After the research and analysis is complete, students put together a presentation for competition with other schools, districts, and states. The highest level of competition is the national contest in June at the University of Maryland. The presentations may be by individual or by a group of up to five students and they may be in the form of written paper (for individuals only), media, performance, or tabletop project (National History Day, 2007).

My comprehensive research (Page, 1992) on National History Day took me all across the country to some interesting places and led me to some fascinating teachers and students. My interview with Phil, an experienced 15-year teacher who had been involved with National History Day for two years, provides this story.

PHIL

The Context

That particular year, the NHD annual theme was "Triumph and Tragedy" and Phil required all of his students to work with other students on their projects; there wouldn't be any individual entries. The reason was a logistical one: Phil had 150 students that year and it would have been too burdensome and probably impossible to monitor and oversee that many individual projects. Phil's students were somewhat homogeneously grouped into what the school, located in a working-class suburb of a large metropolitan area, called the "middle." The students were 98 percent White and 2 percent Black.

Choosing Up

Phil recommended (though this is not necessarily a good plan) that the students choose their own group members. They did so quickly. As usually happens when a teacher asks students to select other students, there was somebody left behind. In this class, Brian and John were the excluded students.

John was a senior who had transferred from another school, and because of different curriculum sequencing at the two schools, had to join the sophomore class in world history. He wasn't happy and tended to stomp around in a sullen mood. Brian suffered from psychological issues and came to school only sporadically. This particular day he was there, and since everyone else had made their choices, John and Brian, who made no attempt to choose anyone at all and whom no one else had chosen, were, by default, left to work together.

The Work (or Lack Thereof)

The district competition was to be in two months and the students worked incredibly hard on their projects; that is, all except for Brian and John. They didn't work at all. Phil persisted with them and required that they stay after school one day, since Brian was actually there, to make some decisions about their project. Brian and John did stay, which was a surprise, but would not speak to each other, so Phil became the language intermediary and liaison. After an hour, they had a topic: Athens and Sparta. John would study Athens and Brian would study Sparta and then at some future time, hypothetically, they would get together and analyze the triumphs and tragedies within and across the two city-states.

A week later, Phil had them stay after school again to see what they had accomplished, which turned out to be nothing at all. But there was another decision, through Phil, made that afternoon that they would make a tabletop presentation for the competition. Another week passed and again nothing had happened. Once again, Phil asked them to stay in the afternoon. Nothing. Finally John brought in a hinged, three-section, 6-foot-high, wooden frame that he had built. He put it in the back of the classroom and there it stayed, as blank as it was on the day he brought it in, until the night before the competition.

The competition was on a Saturday and a bus was to pick up the students and their projects to get them to the district competition, which was taking place in the next town. Phil knew that Brian and John would not be there. The bus came and sure enough, Brian and John did not.

THE CONTEST

The Cadillac

The students set up the tabletop entries in a basement room that had an entire wall of glass that looked out onto and was level with the driveway to the back of the school. Phil was taking photos of his students with their projects when out of the corner of his eye, he saw a car pull up against the glass wall. He knew that car; everyone at the high school knew that car. It was John's car and was a very distinguishable, vintage, black 1957 Cadillac Eldorado with shark fins. Phil didn't know what to think as he watched John get out of the car and open his trunk where the large project frame was visible.

That wasn't the biggest shock. Suddenly the passenger door opened and out jumped Brian. Phil couldn't believe his eyes. These two young men hadn't spoken one word to each other either in class or about the project. Who contacted whom? What did they say to each other? How did they do it? Who decided what? How did this happen? How did they get the project out of the school? Did they actually do something?

The Handshake

They dragged the project out of the trunk and in through the door in the glass wall. Phil, who by this point in the year, had lost patience with the two of them, spoke abruptly to them: "Hurry up and get that on the table. The judges are about to come in."

They put the project on the table. Phil, still in a somewhat sour disposition with them, asked them to stand next to the project (which Phil described as the most "awful attempt at a project" he had ever seen) so that he could take their photo. Brian stood stone faced on one side; John stood with the same lack of affect on the other. No words were spoken. Phil simply asked, "Is that the best you can do?" In the most shocking moment of all, Brian and John simultaneously turned toward each other and, with the slightest of grins, shook hands. That is the photo Phil got.

The Points of This Story

The First Point

The first point that is important in a book on this topic—how to prevent disorder, disruption, and general mayhem in your classroom—is that anytime you make progress, even as small as it seemed with Brian and John, you are on the road to fewer class problems and disruptions and a more stable, well-balanced, exciting, and effective learning environment. Classroom management is not really about disciplining students; it is about managing a classroom full of students so that all are involved, so that disciplining becomes less and less necessary, and so that electric learning takes over as the main activity. It is about preventing, not reacting. It is about being proactive. Managing a class so that students are able to interact and work with others is the biggest step in the right direction. Get your classes to this level and you and everyone else will be able to feel the upbeat, not the fractured and disorderly beat.

The Second Point

The second point is that this story of Brian and John is not a story about failure; it is a story about a huge success. Teaching involves much more than helping students gain mastery or understanding of academic content. If their project was any indication, Brian and John didn't learn a tremendous amount about Sparta or Athens, and there was no analysis in sight. But they did learn something about connecting with another person. In the larger scheme of things, it was a beginning. Actually, considering these two young men, it was monumental.

A Sign That Hung in Einstein's Office at Princeton

Everything that can be counted does not necessarily count; everything that counts cannot necessarily be counted. (as cited in Russo, n.d.)

What counts in this vignette is not what Brian and John accomplished academically, but what they achieved and how they grew as human beings and how their growth then made the heartbeat of the class healthier and stronger, and how the class became less prone to disorder and distraction and more open to learning. Just as Rome was not built in a day, likewise, depending on the particular class and issues, developing student involvement and interaction, and reconstituting and reconstructing a class, can be a slow process—it can take one small step at a time. Developing interaction among students is not always easy. Getting students to work together well and effectively is not always easy, but be assured, those small steps get bigger and faster and as they do, academic learning leaps into high gear. With Phil's persistence, Brian and John had taken those first steps.

THE RESULTS

After the NHD Contest

While students are required to do all their own work on their NHD projects and research, NHD rules allow and encourage students to seek and consider suggestions from others, including the judges. At the district contest described above, one group of Phil's students placed third with their project on the Irish famine. This meant that they would then prepare for and go to the state competition three months later. Phil set up one time slot during the week for the whole class to focus on this winning project.

This was not only a time for all of the students to learn about the triumph and tragedy connected to the Irish famine but also a time to work together in small groups—first, to discuss the academic issues of the famine and how the project represented and could analyze these issues; and second, to develop suggestions on how to improve the project. The three students who had developed the project brought in their changes each week; then they and their peers, under Phil's direction, came together as a large team to discuss possible modifications.

And John and Brian?

Did John and Brian participate? They did, hesitantly and erratically; but they did, especially when in the smaller groups. The project had become a lightening rod of class solidarity and John and Brian had decided, unconsciously or otherwise, by getting themselves to that district competition, that they did want to be involved. The class was on its way to being whole and everyone was part of the heartbeat.

THE ULTIMATE GOAL

As it was for Julia and Phil, the ultimate goal for you is to have a robust and sound rhythm in your class that will crackle and explode with positive student interaction, energy, and learning. The goal is for your class to have a heartbeat that is so healthy and alive that everyone is able to feel that dynamic beat. Students in your class will feel the energy; onlookers will feel it; anyone walking by your room will feel it. Just as you can't teach until everyone is listening, likewise, you can't teach until everyone can feel and is a part of the heartbeat.

SUMMARY: STEP 6

1. Create greater interaction with individual students by having name and eye contact with every student twice every 50- or 60-minute time frame.

2. Develop initial student-to-student interaction by:
   (a) Calling on a second student to elaborate on or question the response (or to respond to a question) from the first student.
   (b) Instructing the second student to respond directly to the first student and not to you.

3. Extend student-to-student interaction by embedding the process in class projects.

4. While increasing interaction, identify and take extra effort with shy and detached students.

5. Remember behavior cues.

6. Feel and embrace the heartbeat of your class.

NOW WHAT?

You now have all of the Six Simple Steps with which to create a safe, positive, alive, and jumping classroom, one which is noteworthy for fiery, productive energy but not disorder. It's never too late. Whether you are in a practicum or are a first-year teacher or you have been teaching for 25 years, if you want to change your classroom, you can. If you think that your class is in too much chaos or disarray to try to implement even one of these steps, take a look at Chapter 7, "Harry and Clara Reclaim Their Classes." You should find some ideas there on how to begin all over again with your class(es).

7

Harry and Clara Reclaim Their Classes

HARRY

The Context

I met Harry when I became his supervisor as he began his student teaching practicum. He was smart, loved history, and was excited to begin this experience in which he eventually would be teaching two classes of world history and two classes of United States history. The classes were a mix of juniors and sophomores. The high school was in a middle to upper-middle class, suburban city of approximately 40,000. The city's population was 95 percent White. Harry's classes were entirely White.

During the first several weeks, Harry spent time observing, getting to know the students, creating plans, and teaching some classes. For this time period, the mentor teacher was in the room with him. Predictably, when the mentor teacher left the classes in Harry's hands, the students' behavior deteriorated. But, it is essential that student teachers establish themselves as the leader in the class and to do that, the mentor teacher has to leave the room for a sustained period of time. Harry seemed to be making progress, but when I made my fifth observation visit, something happened in one of his classes that almost torpedoed his career.

Harry's Full Classroom

The class was completely full. Every desk and chair held a student, some so big that they looked forever stuck in the chairs that were attached to the desks. Not only were all the seats full and stuffed, there seemed to be an extra row jammed into the room. There was little space to walk up the aisles. The only place for me to sit was on the radiator at the windows in the back corner of the room, where I also set up the video camera. Harry was reviewing content with the class for an upcoming test and he was standing at a wall map pointing out and marking locations as he asked questions.

Harry was particularly proud of the plastic covering he had found for the pull down map. The cover allowed students to write with markers to indicate routes, locations, and directions. For a while, students were attending and responding to Harry's questions. He was calling on students by name, but his questioning went on for way too long and as the engagement of the class started to wane, trouble started to bubble up. At one point a student sitting fairly close to me made a rude noise while another student was responding to one of Harry's questions. Harry became noticeably shaken. It didn't help that I was in the room and videotaping the class.

HARRY'S MISTAKE: AN ULTIMATUM

"The next person who makes a noise will go to the principal's office," Harry declared with as much bravado as he could generate. Most teachers know that if you are going to make an ultimatum (not a recommended practice in any situation), you have to be able to follow through on the threat. Harry had done it. It was too late to undo it. And within 30 seconds, as he continued the class, another student made a loud "Moo-o-o-o" like a cow. With no other alternative, since he had already made the threat, Harry ordered the student to go to the office. As the student tried several times to argue with Harry, Harry each time simply repeated, "Go to the office." Fortunately, Harry knew not to get into an argument with a student. That is always a losing proposition. But Harry was even more visibly shaken at this point. Thankfully, the class ended five minutes later.

HARRY'S MELTDOWN AND RECOVERY

That night I received a phone call from Harry. He told me he had gone home from school that day and could not stop vomiting. He had made a decision not to return to the school and would forfeit his work, grade, and certification. After some time in conversation, I convinced Harry to return to school the next day and at least talk to the mentor teacher. He did do this and after a very long discussion, Harry and the mentor teacher put together a proposal for rectifying the class-room situation. It is this process that I recommend you use, and adapt to your own situation, if you believe your class has gotten to the point of no return in terms of classroom disarray.

THE LETTER

Harry and the mentor teacher agreed that Harry would send the students in the class a letter about the situation. In the letter to the students, Harry explained that the discourtesy, the noises, and the interruptions that had occurred in the class were not acceptable and not conducive to a civil or effective learning environment. He told the students that he cared about their academic and social well-being and asked them to help him discover the causes of, and to help solve, the problems in the class.

Harry prompted each student to write him a letter of response. Students were to describe their thoughts on the situation and analyze their own actions. What is important here is the process—the process of involving the students in solving a class problem and of giving the students a voice.

THE STUDENTS' RESPONSES

The students wrote the response letters to Harry and he in return sent the letters back with a personal note attached. Not only did Harry learn what the students thought, but he learned a lot about himself, a lot about the classroom dynamic, and a lot about adolescents in general. There were three main themes in these student letters.

The First Theme

The first theme was one of apology for causing Harry distress and emotional damage. Most of the students who wrote letters of apology did not see that they had caused any of the problems, but did apologize on behalf of the class. Some of these letters were overly solicitous and overly complimentary to Harry and most blamed the problems on the immaturity of a few students. Except for two of these letters, those representing this first theme were all from the young women in the class. Solutions from this group of letters ranged from suggesting that the students try to do better to recommending that Harry give detentions and even use corporal punishment.

The Second Theme

The second prominent theme was one of a half-hearted apology along with pronounced defensiveness. Some of these students claimed that Harry was picking on them or that he was punishing the class for the behavior of a few. All of these letters came from the young men in the class and one young woman, who blamed the problems on overcrowding, the class being too close to lunch time, and the fact that no one wanted to be in a classroom anyway. Suggestions from this group were that Harry explain things more clearly, not take things so seriously, not pick on students, punish only those students who misbehaved, and get advice from a real teacher.

The Third Theme

Five of the letters, three from the first group and two from the second, also focused on the fact that Harry was a student teacher and that, in general, students don't give student teachers the respect they deserve.

And Max

Max, the student Harry had sent out of the room, wrote a one sentence letter that summed up his idea of both the problem and solution; he ordered Harry to learn how to teach.

THE RESULTS

The results for Harry were positive. He didn't have a long time left in the class before the end of the semester, but the student behavior changed in a positive way after the letters. It wasn't so much what was in the letters that was important, as that they had allowed the students to have a voice. What Harry had learned from these letters was invaluable. In addition, Harry's responses to their letters showed the students that he cared about them and really did want things to be better in the class, and that he would pay attention to their ideas. And since the time that Harry tried this experiment, other student, novice, and veteran teachers have tried this approach and have had the same affirmative results; that is, the process led to teacher and students starting over and changing the unhealthy, unsafe, often chaotic, and unproductive classroom dynamic.

Streamlining Harry's Format

If Harry's open-ended letter request leaves you feeling too vulnerable, there is another way to request student input in a more controlled way. Print two unfinished statements allowing half a sheet of paper for the response to each.

Statement 1: What I like the best about this class is:

Statement 2: What I would change about this class if I were the teacher is:

The second statement requires that the students take responsibility for thinking positively about changes and usually eliminates negative or inappropriate student responses. There is always the chance of an outlier response, but it is easily recognizable as such. Even that kind of response can give you much insightful and helpful information about a particular student.

In lower grades, teachers have used Harry's approach as well but instead of asking the students to write a letter about the problem, the teachers have asked the students to draw a picture or series of pictures about the problems.

Clara

The Context

Clara was a student teacher in a second-grade class of 25 students in what was considered a progressive elementary K–5 school in a suburban town of approximately 7,600 people, 98 percent of which were White. For the first two weeks of Clara's practicum, she was to observe the class and to get to know the students and the class procedures. During her second week, I made the first supervisory visit to introduce myself and to review the practicum requirements with Clara. I sat next to Clara in the back of the classroom as we together observed student misbehavior and teacher response.

The Problem

Students were off task, some were shooting elastic bands through the air, some were pulling or braiding each other's hair; some had their heads on their desks. That was some of what was happening. The teacher threatened the students that each time someone misbehaved, she would draw a part of a face on the board. If the face was complete, then the whole class would miss recess. A paper plane flew and landed near the teacher's desk—she drew the first eye. One of the boys started to laugh about something another had said—she drew the second eye. A girl shrieked as her neighbor kicked her— the teacher drew the nose. Yes, the face soon was complete.

Clara looked at me in horror, not knowing what to do or think. But this wasn't the end of the misbehavior or the end of the teacher's reactions. Whatever the next student indiscretion was, the teacher ordered all students to put their work in their desks, to put their heads down on the desk tops, and to stay there until a bell rang. The teacher set a giant timer on her desk. Tick, tock; tick, tock; tick, tock. This was particularly interesting because as the teacher sat at her desk thinking the students were now behaving, Clara and I saw about ten elastic bands zooming around. Clara was clear that these punishments were not the way to establish order or an environment for learning in the class and in fact were daring the students to misbehave more.

Clara's Approach

Drawings

Clara was to begin teaching this class the following Monday and was petrified of these second graders. How could she handle these students? What could she do to get these students back on track and engaged in learning? We talked about the approach Harry had taken with his class and I asked Clara how she could adapt that approach to this second grade. It was Clara's idea to begin her first day by asking the students to draw what they liked best about their class and what they would like to change about their class. The teacher approved this plan, thankfully.

What the Students Wanted to Change

Clara and the teacher learned as much from the drawings as Harry had learned from the letters. The drawings that responded to what the students would like to change about their class included several of the face the teacher had drawn on the board. One student had drawn it and then had drawn lines all across it. One had printed "NO" next to the face. The other drawings that represented desired change were of the misbehaviors in the class—several drew pictures of students shooting elastic bands; some drew pictures of one student doing something to another; one drew a picture of one student yanking another off the chair. In one picture, all the misbehaving students were in a big pit. It doesn't take much to translate these drawings.

What the Students Liked

The drawings depicting what they liked in the class included students sitting in a circle reading a book, students working on the computers, and in general, students doing things without distractions or disruptions. Students do not want an unruly class; they don't want mayhem; they also do not want punishments especially when the whole class suffers for the act of one or a few. They want the teacher to lead; i.e., to keep the class safe and to be engaging, knowledgeable, understanding, and caring.

THE RESULTS

Clara's process allowed the same input from students and the same opportunity for the teacher to make responses as had Harry's approach. It had the same positive results. Students began to act in more appropriate ways. Clara explained everything she was doing and why she was doing it. Soon the students settled down and Clara was able to begin implementing the Six Simple Steps to creating a positive and productive classroom environment.

A BONUS: YOU LEARN MORE THAN YOU THINK FROM STUDENT LETTERS OR STUDENT DRAWINGS

Having students write letters to (or draw pictures for) you will do more than give the students a voice and allow them to problem solve with you. The letters and drawings will allow you to learn much more about your individual students, yourself, and your class as a whole than you could imagine. And the more you know about your students and how and what they think, the better able you are to create a safe and positive place for them, but also the easier it is for you to develop and conduct workable, relevant, engaging, and high-level classroom experiences.

It was clear from the students' letters in Harry's class that some students were more mature than others, that some were angry, and that there was a different dynamic among Harry and the female students than there was among Harry and the male students. It was also evident that some students gave Harry little respect or credibility. And in Clara's class, as a result of one very disturbed drawing, the mentor teacher referred one student to the school counselor. What could you learn from letters or drawings from your students?

YOUR TURN

You have the tools, you have the Six Simple Steps, and Harry and Clara have given you strong models of redemption. There is nothing to stop you from eliminating classroom chaos, from being more confident yourself, or from creating the safest, liveliest class imaginable. Chapter 8 discusses how this might work for you.

8

Making This Happen

BEGINNING

There are several different ways to go about making these changes in your classroom and implementing the Six Simple Steps. How you might make this work depends on where you are in your career.

TEACHER PREPARATION COURSES AND PRESERVICE TEACHERS

If you are a preservice teacher, practice with these Six Simple Steps in your teacher preparation courses. This should be the first place the Six Simple Steps occur. Many courses in teacher preparation programs require preservice teachers to develop a lesson plan and conduct one class or more. If it is also a requirement to implement these Six Steps while conducting the class, then you have the opportunity to become familiar with how they work. Even if it is not a requirement, implement them and the professor will think you are a genius. The practice will be invaluable to the whole class.

Another thing you can do is let your professor take a look at this book. There is almost no extra work involved in implementing these steps in the classroom and in teacher preparation classes. The use of these steps provides not only the practice for soon-to-be student teachers but also the opportunity to see how the classroom dynamic changes when these steps are in place and why and how they got developed in the first place. What do you have to lose?

University Professors

Quality Indicators

If you are a university professor unsure of how to assist preservice teachers with classroom management procedures, this process may be helpful. Create a beginning list of characteristics of an exemplary learning experience. In terms of how the preservice teacher is expected to perform when conducting the class, this list may include quality indicators such as *demonstrated understanding of topic, integrated technology, was organized,* and, in the realm of classroom management, *called students by name.* This is just to get the students started. Explain to the students that they will evaluate each other on how well they implement, and *if* they are implementing, these quality indicators as they conduct the class.

Peer Evaluations

After the student has conducted the lesson, he or she will ask the class (calling on students by name) two questions. The language of the questions will always be the same for two reasons: it makes the process consistent for each student and these questions require the responders to take responsibility for suggesting appropriate changes to create a dynamic lesson. This prevents caustic, negative, and unproductive remarks. The questions are:

1. What would have made this learning experience better for you?

2. What worked best for you in this learning experience?

Expanding the List

After this verbal evaluation, the students in the class will then discuss what new quality indicators, in view of the responses to the two questions, need to be on the list in order for the next students' classes to be improved.

This process repeats itself each class, so that each set (assuming two students conduct the class on one day) of subsequent students have a fuller quality indicator list than the previous students had. By the end of the semester, the students are very clear about, and have developed and take ownership for, what constitutes an engaging learning experience and what classroom management techniques and steps need to be in place for that learning experience to be positive and productive. (Yes, the last students to conduct the class have much more responsibility than the first students—as you can guess, many will volunteer to go first.) I will be shocked if the classroom management indicators on the final sheet are not the Six Simple Steps.

STUDENT TEACHERS

At the Beginning of the Practicum

If you had little or no attention to classroom management in your teacher preparation coursework, then this book can become your lifesaver. The trick is to implement these Six Simple Steps from the beginning of your practicum. If you do it then, you can explain all of the processes to the students and can implement at least Steps 1 to 5 simultaneously.

If You Have Already Begun Your Practicum

If you are already part of the way into a practicum and have just discovered this book, it is not too late. It is never too late to make changes to the dynamic in your classroom. If you are not implementing any of these Six Steps or at least not on a consistent basis, and your classroom is not as disturbed or dysfunctional as were those of Harry and Clara, then start with Step 1, explain why you are incorporating the process into your class, how it will work, and what the students' roles will be. When you have mastered that Step, add the next and the next and the next. . . .

If you are already incorporating one or more of these Steps, start with one of the others that you haven't known about and add another as you master that one. If your classroom is wildly out of control and you are feeling like your head is barely above the water, then follow in Harry or Clara's footprints first before you start to implement the Six Steps.

NOVICE TEACHERS

Given that classroom management issues account for the majority of the teachers who leave the profession in the first five years of their career, you may have found this book at a time when you are feeling overwhelmed, frustrated, unable, alone, and ready to quit. If you have already been teaching for a while and don't know what to do next to get your class(es) under control, start with Step 1, explain your changes to the class and reasons for such, master that step and go on to the next one. Continue this process until you have incorporated all steps into your daily activities to the point where they are automatic for you and the class. And spread the wealth. Share this book with another struggling teacher. If you think your class is in too much disarray to incorporate any of these steps, look again at Chapter 7, "Harry and Clara Reclaim Their Classes." Try adapting one of their approaches to your class before you begin with the Six Simple Steps.

Experienced Teachers

It's never, never too late. Whether you have been teaching for 5 years or 25 years, if you want to change your classroom, you can. It will take some persistence to convince your students you are going to apply different processes and procedures in the classroom. You have built a reputation (good or bad) over the last several years and it will take some diligence and focus to show students you mean to sustain the changes. Start with one of the Six Steps, master it, get the students on board and while continuing to implement that step, add the next and continue that process until the procedures are automatic. As with the preservice and novice teachers, if you believe your class is, or classes are, in too much disarray to proceed with these Six Simple Steps, please revisit Chapter 7, "Harry and Clara Reclaim Their Classes," then take a cue from their work and devise a similar process for your own class(es) before beginning to work with the Six Simple Steps.

Bon Voyage

Good luck! You are on your way to creating a classroom free of mayhem, disorder, and disruption: a safe and caring classroom environment which will hum with electric learning and productivity. Take risks. Think outside the box. Remember that asking questions is more important than answering questions. And remember Edward Bear:

> Here is Edward Bear, coming downstairs, now, bump, bump, bump, on the back of his head behind Christopher Robin. It is, as far as he knows, the only way of coming downstairs, but somewhere he feels there is another way, if only he could stop bumping for a moment and think of it. (Milne, 1926, p. 1)

Appendix

Handling Unwanted
and Inappropriate Responses

It will happen. When you move away from asking the same reliable, though class controlling, four or five students, you will have to handle unwanted, inappropriate, and unexpected responses. Some students will want to test you. Some simply won't know the answer, and won't want to look stupid, so instead of answering incorrectly or saying they don't know, will lapse into clownlike behavior—that is more acceptable to peers. Some students, with no ulterior motives, will give incorrect responses; some won't want you to bother them, so will continue to give inappropriate responses until you stop calling on them. (Now, who is in control?)

The best way to avoid all of these unwanted and unexpected responses is to have students work in pairs. Give every pair a chance to finish writing an answer or solving a problem. Once every pair has finished, you know that you can call on any student. Everyone has an answer and no longer will feel so vulnerable. If this process won't work with your students or in certain situations, then you have to be ready for and have comments for unwanted student responses. Most responses will be variations of the following four examples.

EXAMPLES

First is the student response, then the teacher's:

1. Student: "I don't know."
   What the teacher can do:
   - First, slow down. Maybe the student does know but is just unsure.
   - Work with the student; rephrase the question in different ways; provide some cues to the student.
   - Ask another student to assist—have the second student make verbal and eye contact with the first student, not with you. Return to the first student and check for understanding again.

2. Student: "I think it's north of Chicago." [It's not correct.]
   What the teacher can do:
   - Exactly as in #1.

3. Student (in a sullen tone): "Who cares." [It's not a question.]
   What the teacher can do:
   - Very quickly respond with, "I care, Jonathan. Let's figure it out."
   - It would be rare for a student to not cooperate at this point.
   - But, it may take more conversation about how you care about every student and how you need to know if anyone is having trouble understanding.

4. [Brace yourself] Student: "This class s——s. I am getting out of here." [The student throws books on the floor and slams the door while rushing out of the room.]
   What the teacher can do:
   - First, it happens. Get ready for it.
   - Second, you need to inform the office immediately that a student has left your classroom. If there is an intercom, use that. Be extremely composed. Don't go

into detail. That will come later. If there is no intercom, very quickly write it down on a piece of paper, staple the paper closed, and calmly ask a reliable student to take the note to the office.

- Third, speak to the class quietly and calmly. This behavior will have upset them as well as you, but you have to be the cool one. Let the students know everything is under control and the class will get back to what it was doing.

These are the most common unwanted responses. There are probably others, but none need to cause classroom catastrophe. Your job is to involve everyone in the classroom activity and once you get comfortable responding to these kinds of student responses, you will be less hesitant to call on marginal students.

References

Alder, N. I., & Moulton, M. R. (1998). Caring relationships: Perspectives from middle school students. *Research in Middle Level Education Quarterly, 21*(3), 15–32.

Alliance for Excellent Education. (2005, August). Teacher attrition: A costly loss to the nation and to the states. *Issue Brief.* Retrieved March 2, 2008, from http://www.all4ed.files/archive/publica tions/TeacherAttrition.pdf (Search "teacher attrition")

Bandura, A. (1986). *Social foundations of thought and action: A social cognitive theory.* Englewood Cliffs, NJ: Prentice Hall.

Bandura, A. (1996). Multifaceted impact of self-efficacy beliefs on academic functioning. *Child Development, 67,* 1206–1222.

Banks, J. A. & Banks, C. A. M. (Eds.). (2004). *Handbook of research on multicultural education* (2nd ed.). San Francisco: Jossey-Bass.

Beane, J. (1997). *Curriculum integration: Designing the core of democratic education.* New York: Teachers College Press.

Bergan, M. (2007, January 25). California teacher turnover costs money, expertise. *Capitol Weekly.* Retrieved March 2, 2008, from http://www.capitolweekly.net/article.php?xid=wnom4vplkf4t6b& done=search

Blum, R. W., McNeely, C. A., & Rinehard, P. M. (2002). *Improving the odds: The untapped power of schools to improve the health of teens.* Minneapolis: Center for Adolescent Health and Development, University of Minnesota.

Brophy, J. (1996). *Teaching problem students.* New York: Guilford.

Charles, C. M. (2000). *The synergetic classroom: Joyful teaching and gentle discipline.* New York: Longman.

Christiansen, D. (1996). The professional knowledge-research base for teacher education. In J. Sikula, T. Buttery, & E. Guyton (Eds.), *Handbook of research on teacher education* (2nd ed., pp. 38–52). New York: Simon & Schuster.

Clark, R. J., et al. (1989). *The Math English Science Technology Education Project.* University of Massachusetts, Amherst,

Massachusetts. Project report summary submitted to the Office of Educational Research and Improvement in Washington, DC. (ERIC Document Reproduction Service No. ED 320 895)

Connecticut State Department of Education. (2005). *Handbook for the BEST program for beginning teachers.* Retrieved March 2, 2008, from http://www.sde.ct.gov/sde/search/search.asp?qu=videotaping

Cothran, D. J., & Ennis, C. D. (2002). Building bridges to student engagement: Communicating respect and care for students in urban high schools. *Journal of Research and Development in Education, 33*(2), 106–111.

Cothran, D. J., Kulinna, P. H., & Garrahy, D. A. (2003). "This is kind of giving a secret away . . .": Students' perspectives on effective class management. *Teaching and Teacher Education, 19,* 435–444.

Crosnoe, R., Johnson, M. K., & Elder, G. H. (2004). Intergenerational bonding in school: The behavioral and contextual correlates of student-teacher relationships. *Sociology of Education, 77,* 60–81.

Darling-Hammond, L. (2003). Keeping good teachers: Why it matters, what leaders can do. *Education Leadership, 60*(8), 6–13.

Davis, K. (1999). *A study of beginning teachers' perceptions regarding their teacher preparation programs.* Unpublished master's thesis. University of Minnesota, Minneapolis.

Denzin, N. R., & Lincoln, Y. S. (Eds.). (2005). *The SAGE handbook of qualitative research* (3rd ed.). Thousand Oaks, CA: Sage.

DiGiulio, R. (2007). *Positive classroom management* (3rd ed.). Thousand Oaks, CA: Corwin Press.

Dornbusch, S. M., Erickson, K. G., Laird, J., & Wong, C. A. (2001). The relation of family and school attachment to adolescent deviance in diverse groups and communities. *Journal of Adolescent Research, 16*(4), 396–422.

Emmer, E. T., & Gerwels, M. C. (2006). Classroom management in middle and high school classrooms. In C. M. Evertson & C. S. Weinstein (Eds.), *Handbook of classroom management: Research, practice, and contemporary issues* (pp. 407–438). Hillsdale, NJ: Lawrence Erlbaum Associates.

Ennis, C. D., & McCauley, M. T. (2002). Creating urban classroom communities worthy of trust. *Journal of Curriculum Studies, 34*(2), 149–172.

Evertson, C. M., & Weinstein, C. S. (2006). Classroom management as a field of inquiry. In C. M. Evertson & C. S. Weinstein (Eds.), *Handbook of classroom management: Research, practice, and contemporary issues* (pp. 3–15). Hillsdale, NJ: Lawrence Erlbaum Associates.

Foster, H. L. (1986). *Ribbin', jivin', and playing the dozens: The persistent dilemma in our schools.* Cambridge, MA: Ballinger Publications.

Foundation for a Better Oregon. (2005). Create safe and respectful learning environments. In *Improving Quality and Strengthening Accountability in Oregon's Schools: Fall Report.* Retrieved March 2, 2008, from http://www.chalkboardproject.org/images/PDF/QualityAccountReport.pdf

Gardner, H. (1991). *The unschooled mind: How children think and how schools should teach.* New York: Basic Books.

Geddes, H. (2007). *Attachment in the classroom: The links between children's early experiences, emotional well-being and performance in school.* London: Worth Publishing.

Gee, J. P. (2001). What graduates in education fear most about their first year of teaching. Paper presented at the Annual Meeting of the Louisiana Educational Research Association, Baton Rouge, LA, March 8–9. (ERIC Document Reproduction Service No. ED 454 161)

Hargreaves, A. (2003). *Teaching in the knowledge society: Education in the age of insecurity.* New York: Teachers College Press.

Ingersoll, R., & Smith, T. (2003). The wrong solution to the teacher shortage. *Educational Leadership, 60*(8), 30–33.

Irvine, J. J. (2003). *Because of the kids: Seeing with a cultural eye.* New York: Teachers College Press.

Jay, T. (1996). *What to do when your students talk dirty.* San Jose, CA: Resource Publications.

Jerald, C. D., & Boser, U. (2000). Setting policies for new teachers. *Education Week, 19*(18), 44–45, 47.

Jones, V. F., & Jones, L. S. (2004). *Comprehensive classroom management: Creating communities of support and solving problems* (7th ed.). Boston: Allyn & Bacon.

Kohn, A. (1993). *Punished by rewards: The trouble with gold stars, incentive plans, A's praise, and other bribes.* Boston: Houghton Mifflin.

Labinowicz, E. (1980). *The Piaget primer: Thinking, learning, teaching.* Menlo Park, CA: Addison-Wesley.

Lacina-Gifford, L. (2001). The squeaky wheel gets the oil but what about the shy student? *Education, winter.* Retrieved March 3, 2008, from http://findarticles.com/p/articles/mi_qa3673/is_200101/ai_n8929995

Ladd, K. (2000). A comparison of teacher education programs and graduate's perceptions of experiences. *Dissertation Abstracts International, 1, 61*(12A), 4695 (UMI NO. 9998491).

Marlowe, B. A., & Page, M. L. (2005). *Creating and sustaining the constructivist classroom* (2nd ed.). Thousand Oaks, CA: Corwin Press.

Martin, W. P. (n.d.). *The really big list of classroom management resources.* Retrieved March 3, 2008, from http://drwilliampmartin.tripod.com/classm.html

McCaslin, M., & Good, T. L. (1996). The informal curriculum. In D. Berliner & R. C. Calfee (Eds.), *The handbook of educational psychology* (pp. 622–670). New York: American Psychological Association/Macmillan.

McCormack, C. (2001). Investigating the impact of an internship on the classroom management beliefs of preservice teachers. *The Professional Educator, 23*(2), 1–11.

Milne, A. A. (1926). *Winnie-the-Pooh.* London: Methuen.

Morine-Dershimer, G. (2006). Classroom management and classroom discourse. In C. M. Evertson & C. S. Weinstein (Eds.), *Handbook of classroom management: Research, practice, and contemporary issues* (pp. 127–156). Hillsdale, NJ: Lawrence Erlbaum Associates.

National History Day. (2007). *It's not just a day . . . It's an experience.* Retrieved March 3, 2008, from http://www.nationalhistoryday.org/

Nieto, S. (1999). *The light in their eyes: Creating multicultural learning communities.* New York: Teachers College Press.

Office of the Superintendent of Public Instruction. (2007). *Professional certification handbook.* Retrieved March 3, 2008, from http://www.k12.wa.us/certification/ProfEd/profcertprograms.aspx

Ohanian, S. (2004). On stir-and-serve recipes for teaching. In A. S. Canestrari & B. A. Marlowe (Eds.), *Educational foundations: An anthology of critical readings* (pp. 112–119). Thousand Oaks, CA: Sage.

Orwell, G. (1946). *Politics in the English language.* Retrieved March 3, 2008, from http://www.orwell.ru/library/essays/politics/english/e_polit

Ottavi, T. (2007). *Why is Johnny so detached? A school professional's guide to understanding and helping students with attachment issues.* Chapin, SC: Youthlight, Inc.

Page, M. (1992). *National History Day: An ethnohistorical case study.* Unpublished doctoral dissertation, University of Massachusetts, Amherst.

Page, M. (1999). *Seashore Novice Teacher Professional Certification Pilot Project: Annual report.* Seattle, WA: Seattle University.

Page, M., Simpson, M., & Molloy, P. (2001). *Seashore Teacher Professional Certification Pilot: The clash of a developmental model of teacher performance assessment with a high stakes testing environment and the impact of that clash on novice teachers.* Paper presented at the Annual Meeting of the American Educational Research Association, Seattle, WA, April 10–14. (Eric Document Reproduction Service: No. ED 457 193)

Piaget, J. (1995). Essay on the theory of qualitative values in static sociology. In J. Piaget (Ed.), *Sociological studies* (pp. 97–133). New York. Routledge. (Original work published 1941)

Rosenberg, M., Wilson, R., Maheady, L., & Sindelar, P. (1992). *Educating students with behavior disorders.* Boston: Allyn & Bacon.

Ross, R. P. (1984). Classroom segments: The structuring of school time. In L. W. Anderson (Ed.), *Time and school learning: Theory, research and practice.* London: Croom Helm.

Russo, R. (n.d.). *Albert Einstein quotes.* Retrieved March 3, 2008, from http://www.worldofquotes.com/search.php (Search Einstein)

Salinger, J. D. (1951). *Catcher in the rye.* Boston: Little, Brown.

Schlosser, L. K. (1992). Teacher distance and student disengagement: School lives on the margin. *Journal of Teacher Education, 43*(2), 128–140.

Schneider, B. H. (1992). *Children's social competence in context.* Oxford, UK: Routledge.

Seidman, I. (2006). *Interviewing as qualitative research.* New York: Teachers College Press.

Shin, R., Daly, B., & Vera, E. (2007). The relationship of peer norms, ethnic identity and peer support to school engagement in urban youth. *Professional School Counseling, 10*(4), 379–388.

Supaporn, S. (2000). High school students' perspectives about misbehavior. *Physical Educator, 57*(3), 124–136.

Turiel, E. (1983). *The development of social knowledge: Morality and convention.* Cambridge, UK: Cambridge University Press.

Weinstein, C. S., & Mignano, A. J. (2003). *Elementary classroom management: Lessons from research and practice* (3rd ed.). Boston: McGraw-Hill.

Wentzel, K. R., & Watkins, D. E. (2002). Peer relationships and collaborative learning as contexts for academic enablers. *School Psychology Review, 31*(3), 366–377.

Whitney, L., Golez, F., Nagel, G., & Nieto, C. (2002). Listening to voices of practicing teachers to examine the effectiveness of a teacher education program. *Action in Teacher Education, 23*(4), 69–76.

Winzer, M., & Gregg, N. (1992). *Educational psychology in the Canadian classroom.* Scarborough, ON: Prentice Hall Canada.

Zeidner, M. (1988). The relative severity of common classroom management strategies: The student's perspective. *British Journal of Educational Psychology, 58,* 69–77.

Index

**CORWIN
PRESS**

The Corwin Press logo—a raven striding across an open book—represents the union of courage and learning. Corwin Press is committed to improving education for all learners by publishing books and other professional development resources for those serving the field of PreK–12 education. By providing practical, hands-on materials, Corwin Press continues to carry out the promise of its motto: **"Helping Educators Do Their Work Better."**